PitmanScript SKILL BOOK 1

PitmanScript SKILL BOOK 1

Emily D Smith
BSc Econ (Hons), FRSA

Pitman Publishing

Second edition 1974

Sir Isaac Pitman and Sons Ltd
Pitman House, Parker Street, Kingsway, London WC2B 5PB
PO Box 46038, Banda Street, Nairobi, Kenya

Sir Isaac Pitman (Aust) Pty Ltd
Pitman House, 158 Bouverie Street, Carlton, Victoria 3053, Australia

Pitman Publishing Corporation
6 East 43rd Street, New York, NY 10017, USA

Sir Isaac Pitman (Canada) Ltd
495 Wellington Street West, Toronto 135, Canada

The Copp Clark Publishing Company
517 Wellington Street West, Toronto 135, Canada

ISBN 0 273 00708 4

Text set in 10/12pt IBM Journal Roman, printed by photolithography,
and bound in Great Britain at The Pitman Press, Bath
G4 S.5672:25

Contents

PitmanScript Keys to Dictation Passages

Longhand Keys to Facility Practices

Introductory Notes

The following information and hints will help writers of PitmanScript to reach, in as short a time as possible, their goal of writing with fluency and reading back with complete accuracy.

Paper

Use a notebook with smooth-surfaced lined paper. Cheap paper tends to be thin or 'hairy', and is a deterrent to good and fast penmanship; it is also difficult to write on both sides of poor quality paper.

First go through the notebook using one side of the paper only; you can afterwards work through it again using the backs of the pages. A top-opening notebook (opening quite flat) is preferable to a side-opening exercise book.

Turning the page

This should not be left to chance. Prepare the page in advance by turning up the bottom left-hand corner (the right-hand corner if you are left-handed). As you near the end of the page, hold the corner with the thumb and forefinger of your left (right) hand, and turn the page gently over when you have written the last line.

This page-turning technique is important, because if you fumble at the end of a page you lose valuable seconds. Remember that when writing at 60 words a minute every second represents one word. You cannot afford to overlook the value of such fleeting seconds.

The writing instrument

Since PitmanScript uses a uniform thickness for all strokes and letters, a good-quality ball-point pen (preferably black for clarity) is an excellent medium. Always keep a spare one handy.

While a pencil is quite satisfactory from some points of view, it is not recommended for two reasons – both concerned with lasting quality. In the first place, a pencil point wears down very quickly, leading inevitably to a deterioration in writing. In the second place, pencil notes do not stand up to wear and tear, and can quickly become faint and difficult to read back.

Sitting position

Sit up straight, with both feet on the floor. Try to avoid the tendency to lean over your notebook. Your notebook should be straight in front of you, in line with your writing hand.

Penmanship

Hold your pen very lightly and fairly close to the point. This gives good control, without tension. If you grip hard and press down into the paper, you are handicapping yourself by wasting energy. You need your store of energy to maintain continuous writing and understanding and appreciation of what is being dictated.

Write as lightly as you possibly can. There should be no indentations on the paper; if there are, make an effort to reduce pressure. If you feel yourself beginning to press hard, and your hand is becoming tired, release the pressure and write again as lightly as you can. You will be surprised to find how lightly you can write and what a tiny amount of grip is needed to hold your pen and yet still maintain perfect control over it.

Size of writing

Practise copying the forms given in the *Basic Text* and in this dictation book, writing about the same size as the printed forms. Longhand styles differ: some people write a large and sprawling hand, some use a backward slope. Neither of these is good for PitmanScript. The writing should be either upright or slightly slanting forward; a large sprawling method of writing is a handicap because it takes longer to write and necessitates more turning of pages.

Try to regard PitmanScript as a new form of penmanship, and deliberately cultivate an easy flowing style when writing it.

Facility of writing

In each of the 32 sections of this book there is an exercise in writing facility, which should be practised conscientiously. After reading the PitmanScript forms, you should write each line in your notebook, leaving three or four blank lines underneath it. You should then copy the forms on the blank lines, trying to write more and more quickly and lightly at each repetition.

In any system of fast writing it is the automatic writing of the forms that makes for speed. When you have only an instant in which to hear, understand and reproduce one or more words, there is very little opportunity for thinking how to write: it is essential to write without hesitation. It is familiarity with what has to be written that brings this unhesitating response.

It is recommended that you study and practise the joinings shown in the Tables on pages 103 to 105.

Reading back

As much as possible of what you write from dictation should be read back or typed back. You must, in order to do this, be absolutely familiar with your own style of writing, and you must be conscious of what kind of distortions you make when pressed for time. All fast writers are aware that such distortions occur, so it is better to recognize your own individual ones. The point to remember is that such distortions will become more and more rare as you master the art of writing fast. Try always to read back at least as quickly as you have taken down – more quickly, if possible.

Concentrate on what you are hearing, so that you can follow the meaning of the matter being dictated. This is a great help to rapid transcription, because in this way you make yourself familiar with the subject matter.

Knowledge of words, spelling and meaning

The greater your vocabulary, the easier you will find it to write quickly and read back accurately. A word which puzzles you interrupts the smooth flow of your writing. If you do not understand what is being dictated to you, you will find it twice as difficult to write it accurately. Therefore, when you read books, newspapers and magazines, make sure that you know the meanings of the words used: if you do not understand a word, make a point of looking it up in a dictionary at the first opportunity that presents itself – or *make* that opportunity!

The English language has very definite speech patterns: certain phrases go with other phrases and expressions, and you can become so skilful in your knowledge of these intricate patterns that you can foretell the end of a sentence before the speaker himself has completed it. If you are weak in your mastery and use of words, try to find time to do plenty of reading of a general nature.

Nor must the spelling of words be overlooked. A wrongly spelt word is almost as bad in a letter or document as a wholly wrong one. There are several spelling tests in the course of this book, and they must not be ignored.

700 common words

The words in the list of 700 common words are those that are essential to the framing of correct sentences in English – no matter what subject matter is being dealt with. They are the words which are basic to the language.

The claim made for these 700 words is that they form, with straightforward derivatives, 80 per cent of all everyday written or spoken English. This means that, on average, four out of every five words written in the course of note-taking will be one of the 700 – so you should ensure that you can write all of the common words without hesitation. Any 'thinking time' available to you when writing from dictation can be spent on the less usual words.

Research has shown that the 700 common words (and their derivatives) occur with a frequency of 80 per cent – and even more in some cases – in the speed tests of the various examining bodies. A group of the 700 words and their PitmanScript forms (with alternative advanced forms in many instances) is listed in each section of this book. The forms should be written until you are absolutely familiar with them.

Abbreviating

You need write no more than is necessary to ensure correct reading back. You do not have to write exactly what is written in this book, nor exactly what your neighbour writes. You are the judge of your own requirements.

Initial vowels are always included (except in the case of *x* for *ex-*) so that the writer has a definite indication as to how a word begins. In short words, a final vowel must also be included or indicated.

The longer the word, the less necessary it is to include medial vowels – the consonants are an adequate guide. In words of only one or two syllables, however, it is important to show accented vowels.

A general rule is that it is never necessary to show a medial ĕ (as heard in the word *pen*), or an indistinct vowel (as heard in the second syllable of *mountain* or *stupor*). It is generally satisfactory to omit the short *o͝o* sound heard in such words as *good* and *book*. Another vowel which can safely be omitted, even in short words, is the *o* before *r* in such words as *nor* and *more*; this does not endanger safe reading back because the sounds *ner* and *mer* do not occur in words which conflict in meaning.

In the case of long words, vowels become less important. In the word *part*, for instance, the *a* is shown, but in the word *particular* the first vowel is not stressed and it is not vital to correct reading back. There is the further point that long words need not be written in full: the writer will soon become experienced in representing only parts of more familiar words. For instance, *partic* is adequate for *particular*, *individ* for *individual*, and *pos* or *ps* for *possible*, especially in an expression such as *as soon as possible*. Many short cuts of this kind are used in both written and spoken English, particularly in the advertisements in newspapers.

If you decide on an abbreviation, it is useful to practise saying the word to yourself in its abbreviated form so that you become accustomed to it. Place names, proper names and unfamiliar words need to be written more fully, however.

Links

Forms for words that are linked in speech may be linked in PitmanScript – if you wish to do this. Links are not compulsory, but it is clear that time can be saved in certain cases by such joinings. *As soon as possible*, *more than*, *this is* and *thank you for your letter* are examples of expressions that can usefully be written as links. The links shown in each section of this book are suggestions for time saving, but their use is, of course, optional. If you decide to use the links, you must practise writing them so that you do not hesitate when writing or reading back.

Using PitmanScript

PitmanScript can be written both for business purposes and for personal use. A speed of 80 or 90 words a minute is adequate for most office requirements, provided that the transcription can be made rapidly and accurately. When you are taking down dictation in an office, it is essential for you to follow the meaning of what is being dictated: in other words, take an interest in what you are doing. This will save you from making silly mistakes through misunderstandings.

For private use, PitmanScript is invaluable: it offers a means of making personal notes easily and quickly, whether they are notes for a lecture or report or merely items on a shopping list.

Having learned PitmanScript, use it!

Some notes for teachers

The dictation tests included in this book cover three types of material. In Unit 1, all the tests are restricted to practice in the 700 common words and their derivatives. Each test should be dictated more than once, as the repeated writing of the same form makes the writing become automatic. This is valuable because the writer should, when taking notes, concentrate on the subject matter of the dictation and not on how to write individual forms.

In Unit 2, a vocabulary of 2000 words is used. Here again, repetition is extremely valuable.

Unit 3 consists of a few tests, each containing about 200 words, in which the vocabulary is not controlled or restricted in any way. Because the tests are short, the students can be trained to write and to read the more difficult material contained in them. These tests lead to *PitmanScript Skill Book 2*, which is recommended for the training of students to take the speed tests of the various examining bodies.

All the tests in this first book are counted in tens. The usual method adopted for checking the time of reading is to use a stopwatch or any watch with a clear second hand, and to check the time at each quarter-minute. At 80 words a minute, for instance, 20 words must be read during each 15 seconds.

The clearer and more even the reading, the more confidence and success will students have in their note-taking. If the reader concentrates on the material being read, and clearly conveys its sense to the writer, the writer's task is made easier. Doubt as to what has been said, or confusion as to meaning, diverts attention from the actual note-taking and can lead to gaps in the notes – and therefore in the transcript.

The facility exercises included in each section should be a regular part of class work, and students should be encouraged to practise writing them faster and faster – without loss of clarity.

The PitmanScript notes of the dictation passages can be used for reference purposes, but they should also be used to practise rapid reading, students taking turns at reading short passages at high speed. The alternative advanced forms are used in these passages where appropriate. Familiarity with the forms of PitmanScript is the secret of fast writing and rapid and accurate transcription.

Unit 1

Dictation practice based on the 700 most common words

Vocabulary drill

a/an		**act**	
able		acted	
ably		acting	
about		acts	
above		action	
according		actions	
accordingly		**add**	
account		added	
accounted		adding	
accounting		adds	
accounts		addition	
across		additions	
		additional	

Drill based on Dictation Passage 1

order		ourselves	

position	particular
owing	work
received	workers
supports	held
delivery	better
forward	employed
plans	material
whole	winter
instructions	immediately
difficulty	company
plant	fact

Drill based on links in Dictation Passage 1

Dear Sirs

with regard to*

we regret*

to have to†

inform you

that we find

from you

part of

order of

we were not

very serious

that there would be

led us

for which

we are now

waste of money

will be

have been†

upon us

and we must ask you

at once

yours faithfully

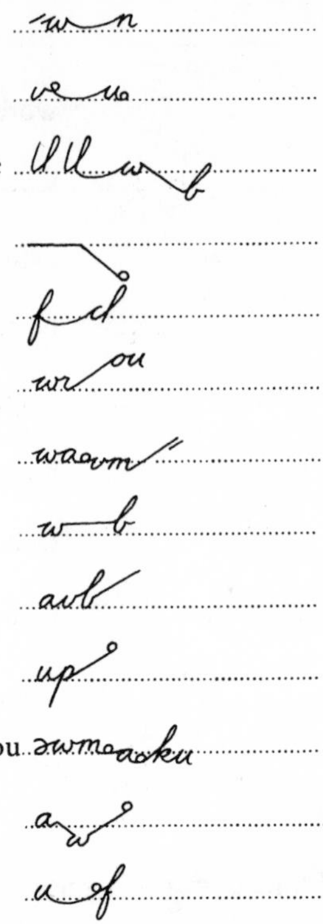

*Note the distinction between these two links.
†The dot for H may be omitted in links, even initially.

Note that the use of links is not compulsory, but as they save the writer time and effort it is advisable to practise and use them.

Dictation Passage 1 (see p. 106 for PitmanScript)

(Letter to the Blackburn Steel Company, City Road, EC1V 1LJ. This letter and the following four form a related set.)

Dear Sirs, With regard to our order B396[10] we regret to have to inform you that we[20] find ourselves in a very serious position owing to our[30] not yet having received from you the two M.S.[40] supports, marks B3 and 4, which formed part of[50] our order of April last.

Your early delivery of the[60] other parts of this order and the fact that we[70] were not told by you that there would be any[80] difficulty about the delivery of these two supports led us[90] to go forward with the plans for completing the whole[100] plant. We gave instructions to other companies to carry out[110] their particular parts of the work, and these companies now[120] find their work held up for want of the supports.[130] This hold-up is causing waste of money both to[140] us and to the other companies, and the workers would[150] have been better employed on other work for which material[160] was ready. With winter upon us we are now in[170] a serious position, and we must ask you to wire[180] immediately that the supports will be sent at once. Yours[190] faithfully, (191)

Where single letters such as M.S. are dictated, it is better to write them with the ordinary small alphabetic symbols, as this makes writing faster and reading back easy.

Facility Practice 1 (see p. 134 for Key)

(a) 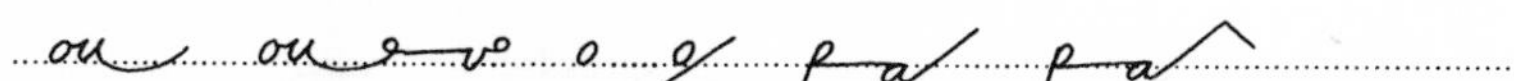

(b) 

(c) 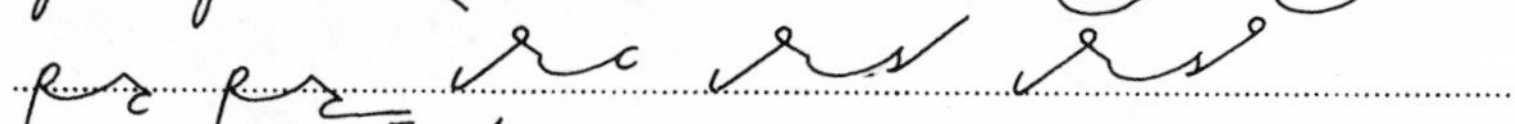

(d) 

(e) 

(f) 

Vocabulary drill

advantage	**age**
advertise	aged
advertised	ageing
advertising	ages
advertises	**ago**
advertisement	**agree**
advertiser	agreed
after	agreeing
afterwards	agrees
afternoon	agreeable
again	agreeably
against	disagreeable
	agreement

Drill based on Dictation Passage 2

officially	trouble
outstanding	between
personally	products
really	business
eyes	methods

influence	uf	improve	imp v
		situation	sy

Notice that it is not necessary to include all vowels.

Drill based on links in Dictation Passage 2

Dear Mr Weeks	mwks	I shall be very pleased	is bvp
we have	wav	very much	vmcl
I have a	iava	between us	bw
to tell you	t u	if you will	ufuw
want of this	w vlf	yours truly	u

Dictation Passage 2 (see p. 107 for PitmanScript)

(Personal letter to Mr F Weeks of the Blackburn Steel Company)

Dear Mr Weeks, With regard to our order B396[10] we have sent to you officially today a[20] letter about the two M.S. supports which are still[30] outstanding. I am writing this note to you personally to[40] tell you that we are really in a bad hole[50] for want of this material, and only immediate delivery of[60] the supports will save your company in the eyes of[70] this company. I very much regret this trouble between us,[80] as I have a liking both for your products and,[90] up till now, for your business methods. I shall be[100] very pleased, therefore, if you will use your personal influence[110] to improve the situation. Yours truly, (116)

Facility Practice 2 (see p. 134 for Key)

(a) ofs ofs ofs ou ou

(b) p p p p

(c) b bw imp v imp v imp v s s

(d) iav wav is f ws f vg vp vmcl

Vocabulary drill

air
airplane
airplanes
airs
airy
all
almost
already
although
always
along
also
altogether
am
among
amongst
amount
amounts
amounting
and
animal
animals

Drill based on Dictation Passage 3

customers
number
placed
late
regard
importance
quickly
full
satisfactory
answer
we sent you a
you will see
and you must
so that
we can

Dictation Passage 3 (see p. 107 for PitmanScript)

(Letter from the Blackburn Steel Company to their Works)

Dear Sirs,

Our Order 92/57: Customers'[10] *Order No B396*

We sent you a[20] wire today regarding this order. We are placed in a[30] very serious position with customers in the matter of the[40] late delivery of supports, marks B3 and 4, as[50] you will see from the copy of letter sent with[60] this.

It is of first importance that we get the[70] supports delivered quickly, and you must regard this work as[80] coming before all other work.

When writing, please give us[90] full particulars of the cause of the late delivery, so[100] that we can give our customers a satisfactory answer. Yours[110] faithfully, (111)

Facility Practice 3 (see p. 134 for Key)

(a) 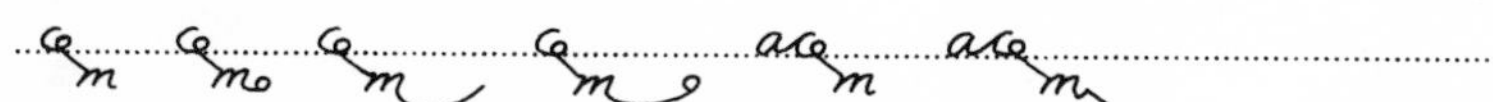

(b) 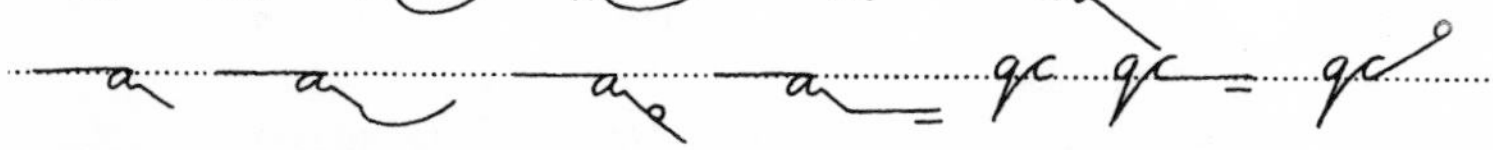

(c) 

(d) 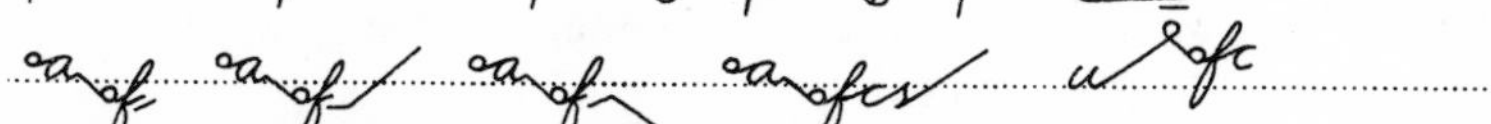

(e) 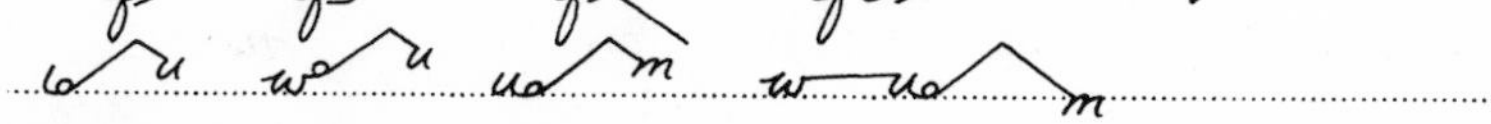

(f) 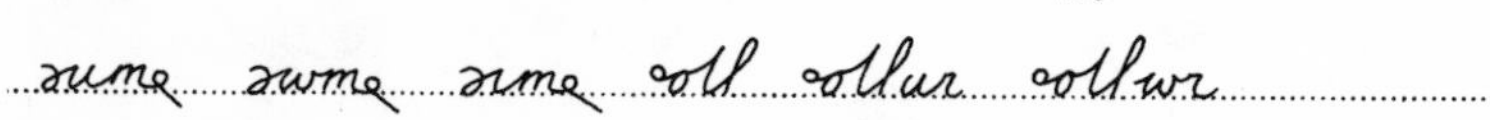

Spelling: Remember to repeat the underlined consonants in the following words when writing longhand: accommodation, embarrass, parallel, occurrence, all right, marvellous. A letter or document with spelling errors is not acceptable, however neat and accurate it may be in other respects. The PitmanScript forms for these words are:

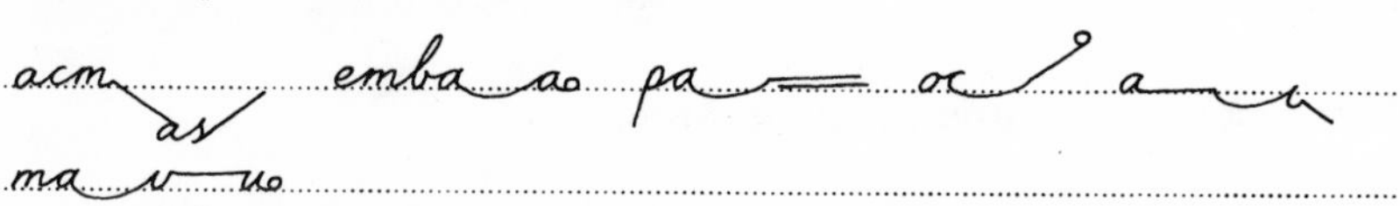

The consonants are not repeated in PitmanScript because they are sounded once only.

Vocabulary drill

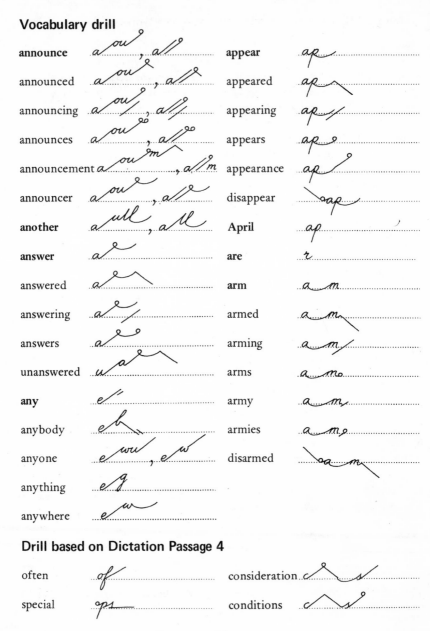

announce	**appear**
announced	appeared
announcing	appearing
announces	appears
announcement	appearance
announcer	disappear
another	**April**
answer	**are**
answered	**arm**
answering	armed
answers	arming
unanswered	arms
any	army
anybody	armies
anyone	disarmed
anything	
anywhere	

Drill based on Dictation Passage 4

often	consideration
special	conditions

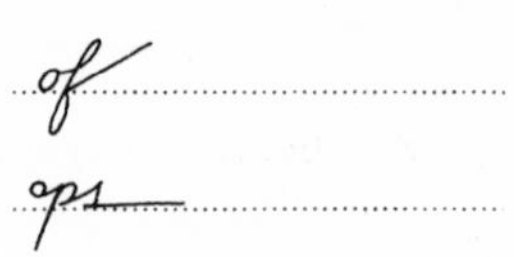

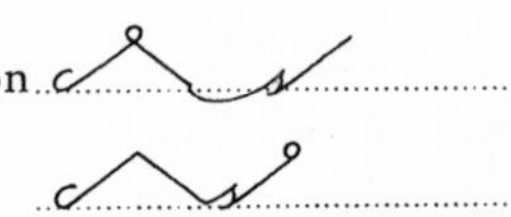

demand	in this case
quite	we get
necessary	in our
otherwise	may have to
cannot	well worth
important	next week
public	next week or two
profitable	look forward
additional	and to seeing the
within	I hope to be
Dear Mr Power	who have
you know that	to having
I do not	which has been

Dictation Passage 4 (see p. 107 for PitmanScript)

(Covering letter to Mr Power at the Works sent with previous letter)

Dear Mr Power, You know that I do not often[10] call for special consideration for any particular customer, but in[20] this case conditions demand it. It is quite necessary that[30] we get these supports delivered immediately; otherwise customers cannot keep[40] to dates given to important public officials, and we in[50] our turn may have to face the loss of customers[60] who have given us good and profitable work.

A little[70] additional cost in getting these supports away quickly will be[80] well worth while. I hope to be at the Works[90] within the next week or two, and look forward to[100] having a talk with you and to seeing the new[110] plant which has been put in. Yours truly, (118)

Facility Practice 4 (see p. 135 for Key)

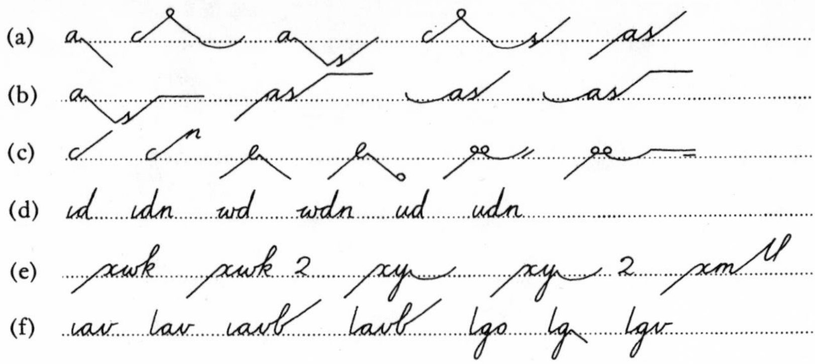

Note: It is important to distinguish between *you* and *we*: ur = *you are*, wr = *we are*, ud = *you do*, wd = *we do.*

Vocabulary drill

art	**attention**
arts	attend
artful	attended
as	attending
ask	attends
asks	**August**
asked	**authority**
asking	authorities
at	authoritative
attempt	authoritatively
attempts	**away**
attempting	
attempted	

Drill based on Dictation Passage 5

weekend	difficulty
Monday	respect
reach	did
morning	wrong
already	size

means	to take*
outweighs	we take*
we wired you	which is not
stating that	no doubt
we thought	owing to

* The vowel is omitted if the meaning is obvious.

Dictation Passage 5 (see p. 108 for PitmanScript)

(Letter from Works to Head Office)

Order 92/57. We wired you today[10] stating that delivery of supports B3 and 4 will[20] be made on Tuesday. Men will work this weekend, and[30] we have no doubt that the work will be ready[40] by Monday afternoon. The supports will be sent by road,[50] and should reach customers by Tuesday morning. We have to[60] inform you that these two supports were not of the[70] same size as the supports already delivered. They had to[80] be got specially and, as you know, there are many[90] difficulties at present in this respect.

When the material did[100] come to hand the supports were cut to the wrong[110] size owing to wrong marking. We regret that you were[120] not informed of this at the time. We are still[130] waiting for delivery of material, but after getting your wire[140] we thought it best to take material from order[150] 87/31, which is not required immediately.

This[160] means a certain amount of waste but we take it[170] that the importance of early delivery outweighs other considerations. (179)

Facility Practice 5 (see p. 135 for Key)

(a)

(b)

(c)

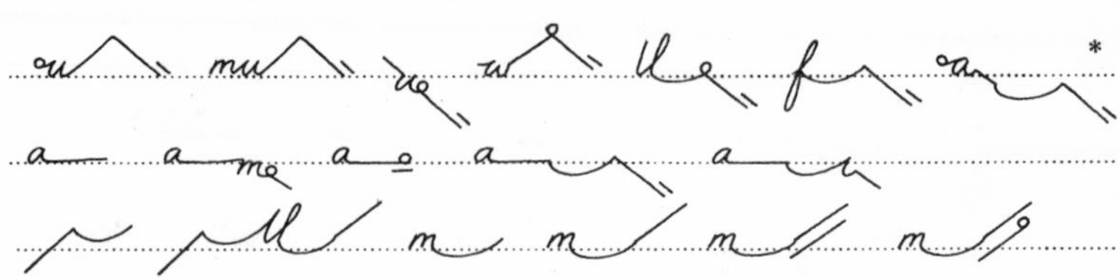

(d) 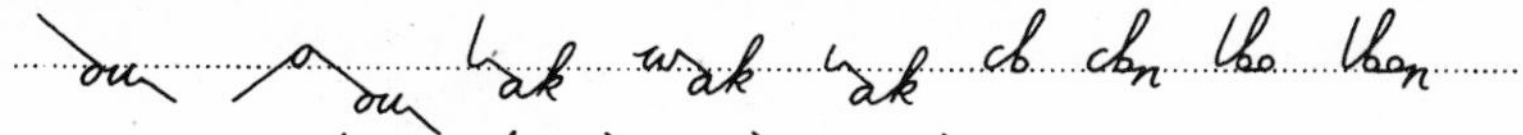

(e) 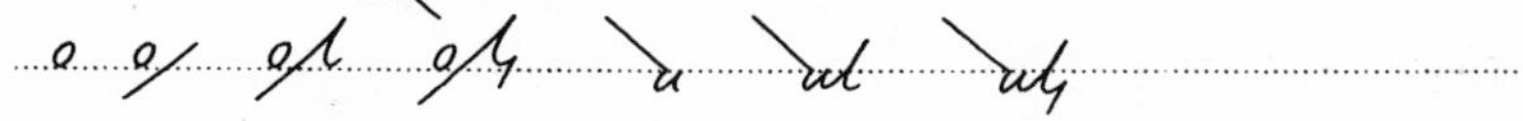

*If preferred the abbreviations often employed in longhand may be used, representing only *Sun*, *Mon*, *Sat*, etc. Alternatively, vowels may be omitted:

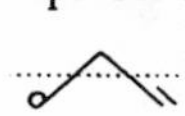 *Sunday*, 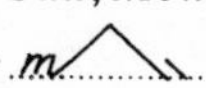 *Monday*, etc.

Spelling: Remember to repeat the underlined consonants in the following words when writing longhand: o<u>cc</u>upy, i<u>mm</u>igrate, i<u>nn</u>ate, i<u>nn</u>ovate, a<u>pp</u>reciate, a<u>pp</u>roximate. In PitmanScript one consonant only is used for the single sound:

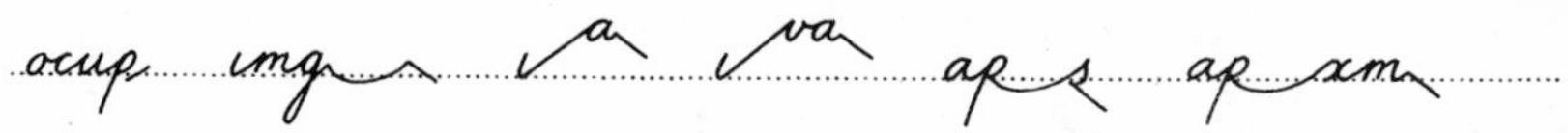

See page 15 for revision of other examples.

Vocabulary drill

baby
babies
babyish
back
backed
backing
backs
backward
background
bad
badly
balance
balanced
balancing
balances

bank
banked
banking
banks
base
based
basing
bases
basic
basically
basis

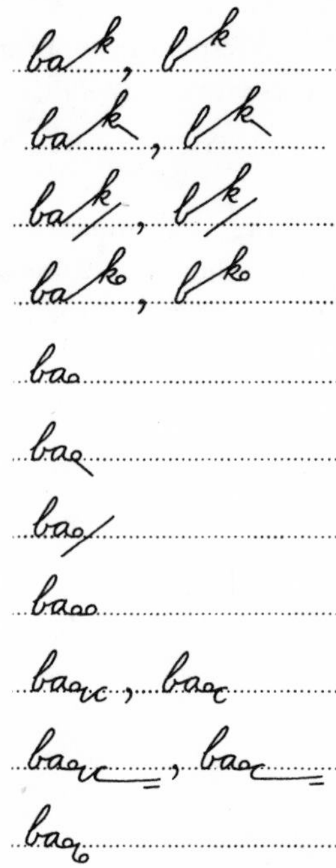

Drill based on Dictation Passage 6

home
manufacture

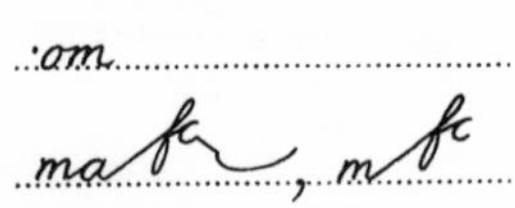

manufacturing
Riverside

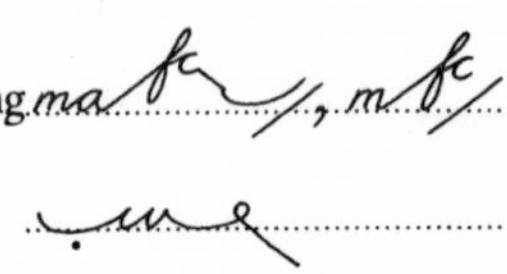

kindly	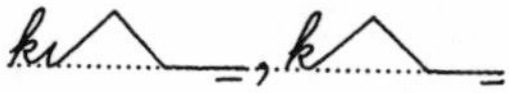	will you	
list	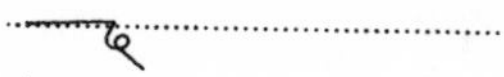	price list	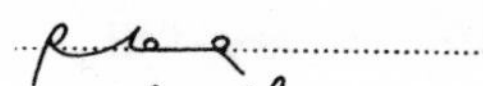
details	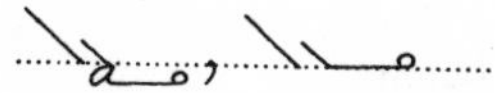	in this month's	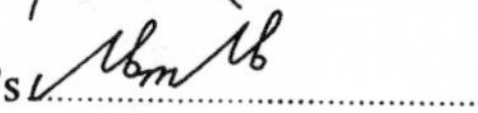
different	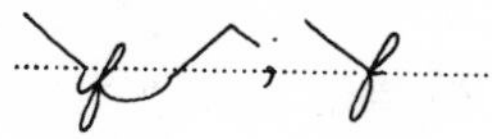	of your	
paper	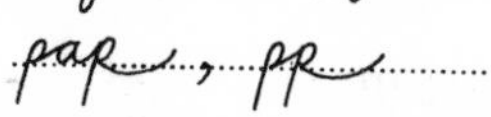	inform us	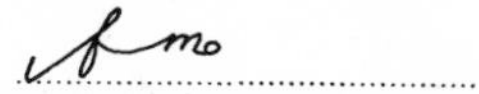
whether	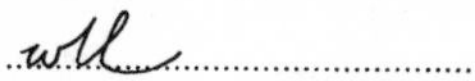	we are	
country	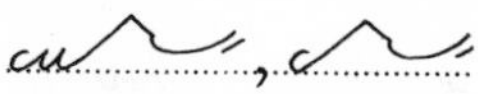	very truly yours	
showrooms	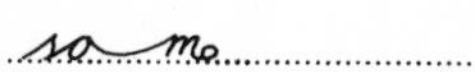		

Dictation Passage 6 (see p. 109 for PitmanScript)

(Letter to the Home Manufacturing Company, Riverside. Dictation Passages 6–9 form a related set.)

Dear Sirs, Will you kindly send us an up-to-[10]date price list, giving details of your different lines in[20] small tables, as advertised in this month's issue of your[30] trade paper. When writing, will you please inform us whether[40] you have any showrooms in this part of the[50] country. Hoping to receive an early answer, We are, Very[60] truly yours, (62)

Facility Practice 6 (see p. 135 for Key)

(a) 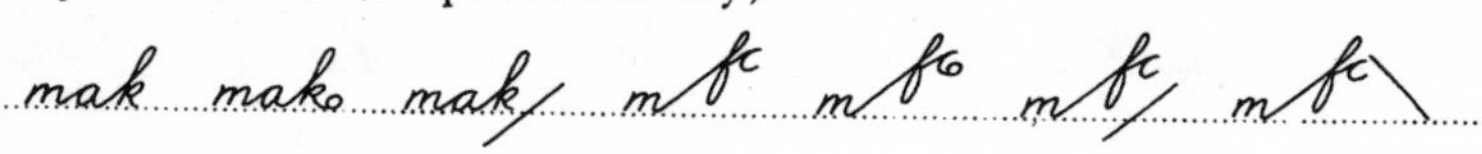

(b) 

(c) 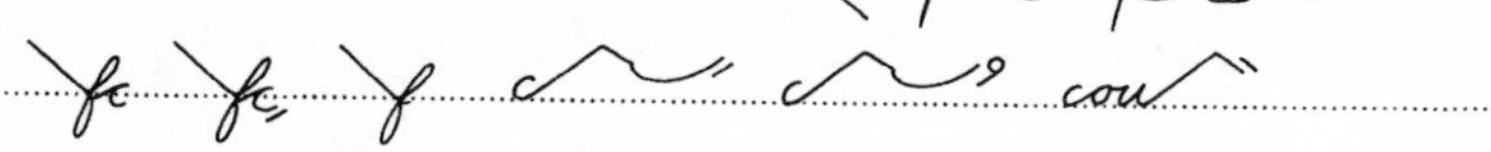

(d) 

Vocabulary drill

be
beautiful
beautifully
because
become
becomes
became
bed
beds
before
begin
began
begun
beginning
begins
behind
belief
beliefs
believe
believed
believing
believes

Drill based on Dictation Passage 7

services
gentlemen
colours
nothing
purposes
requirements
fully
either
chief
experience
however
large

water	wau, w
interested	
we have to thank you	wav la ku
for your letter	fu
we have to thank you for your letter	wav la kuf
we should	ws
of course	vc
to your	lu
what is	ws
as to the	ao
we shall be	ws b
yours respectfully	u e spc
we are able to	wrab
to be put	lbp

Dictation Passage 7 (see p. 109 for PitmanScript)

(Letter to Personal Services, North Wells)

Gentlemen, We have to thank you for your letter, which[10] reached here this morning. We are sending you today our[20] price list, which gives details of sizes, colours and prices[30] of the many different kinds of table which we are[40] able to supply on demand. Should there be nothing in[50] this list to meet your particular purposes we should, of[60] course, be ready to manufacture goods specially to your requirements.[70] As you do not state in your letter the use[80] to which the tables are to be put, we cannot[90] at the moment direct your attention to any particular line,[100] and we should like you to write to us more[110] fully in this respect.

We regret to inform you that[120] we have no showrooms either in your town or[130] in any nearby town. The only showroom we have,[140] in addition to that in our chief Works, is in[150] the south, where we experience our biggest demand. If, however,[160] you will look through the list now sent to you[170] and write to us again, giving us your opinion regarding[180] what is offered and informing us as to the purpose[190] for which the tables are required, we shall be quite[200] willing to send you large-size water-colours of any[210] tables in which you are interested, showing the colour and[220] other details. Yours respectfully, (224)

Facility Practice 7 (see p. 135 for Key)

(a) 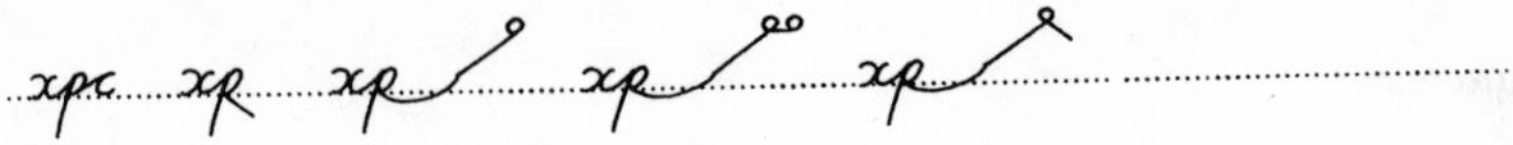

(b) 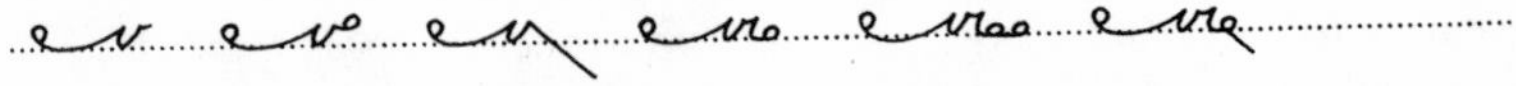

(c) 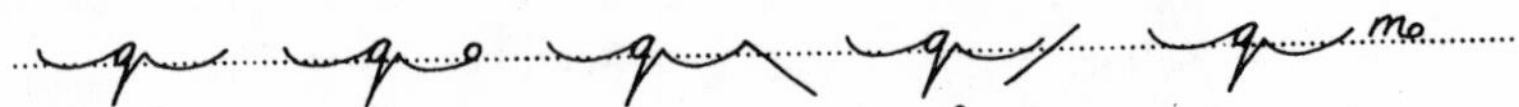

(d) 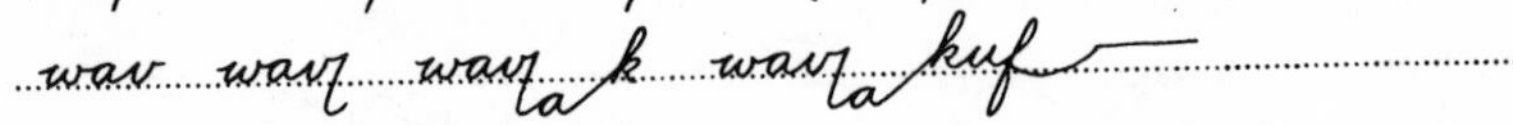

(e) 

Vocabulary drill

best		**board**	
better		boarded	
between		boarding	
beyond		boards	
big		**body**	
bigger		bodies	
biggest		bodily	
black		**book**	
blacker		booked	
blackest		booking	
blackness		books	
blue		**both**	
bluer		**bought**	
bluest			

Drill based on Dictation Passage 8

carefully		front	
acting		judge	
house		weight	
lower		iron	

measure	ms	we have now	wav ou
measuring	ms	in our opinion	ou op
anything	eg	in this connection	lbc c
question	qs	so far as	sofa s
suggestion	gs	we should be	ws b
April	ap	we must have the	wms av

Dictation Passage 8 (see p. 109 for PitmanScript)

(Letter to the Home Manufacturing Company, Riverside)

Dear Sirs, We have now considered carefully the details of[10] tables given in your price list, and in our opinion[20] Line C is the line most likely to meet our[30] requirements. We are acting for two gentlemen who own a[40] large house in the country and who are planning to[50] open the lower front part of the house to the[60] public, serving light meals. It is in this connection that[70] the tables are required. So far as we can judge,[80] the tables shown under Line C, numbers 10 and 10a,[90] are of the right size and weight. Can you[100] supply on demand fifteen No 10 tables in light blue[110] and gold, and fifteen No 10a tables in a[120] plain deep blue? If so, will you kindly send, as[130] offered, a water-colour of the tables in these colours[140] – or, better still, send us a table of each kind[150] so that we may know just what we should be[160] buying.

We are also interested in a table for out-[170]door use, with a strong iron base. Those shown in[180] your list are not, however, of the right kind, being[190] too small and light. We should like a round table[200] of good quality and heavy weight, measuring from two and[210] a half to three feet across. Can you offer anything[220] of this kind? We should like an early answer, as[230] if the gentlemen in question go forward with the suggestion[240] we must have the rooms open and in perfect running[250] order by the second weekend in April. Yours truly, (259)

Note: The joining *ir* is kept distinct from *cr*, as follows: ir = *iron*; cs = *course.*

Facility Practice 8

Figures are generally written with the numerals:

1 2 3 4 5 6 7 8 9 0

It is important to write numbers very clearly, and the following drill gives practice in this. The figure for *six* must be carefully distinguished from *zero*, and the figure for *one* from that for *seven*, as:

60 17

When the word *one* is used as a noun, pronoun or adjective, it is better to write wu/ or w/, as:

wu/ vus or w/^vs = *one of us*

a g wu/ or a g w/ = *a good one*

(a) 1 3 5 7 9 2 4 6 8 0

(b) 1 7 7 1 0 6 6 0 1 7 6 0

As it is a waste of time to write a series of zeros, *hundred* may be represented by /, *thousand* by U, and *million* by m, as in line (c) which follows:

(c) 3/ 3U 3m 3/U 3/m 3Um

Vocabulary drill

boy	**bread**
boys	**bring**
boyhood	bringing
boyish	brings
brake / **break**	brought
braking / breaking	**brother**
brakes / breaks	brothers
broke	**build**
broken	building
	builds
	builder
	built

Drill based on Dictation Passage 9

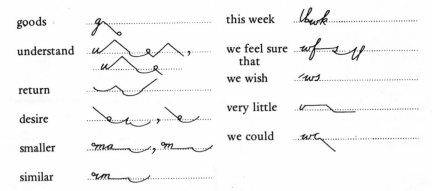

goods	this week
understand	we feel sure that
return	we wish
desire	very little
smaller	we could
similar	

Dictation Passage 9 (see p. 110 for PitmanScript)

(Letter to Personal Services, North Wells)

Gentlemen, We have today sent to you by goods train[10] the two tables which you ask to see. These should[20] reach you before the end of this week. We feel[30] sure that you will like these tables, but we wish[40] you to understand that you are quite free to return[50] them, at our cost, if they are not what you[60] desire. We can supply these tables in large numbers on[70] demand.

As for the tables with heavy iron base, there[80] is very little demand for these now. We could, however,[90] offer you right away six round tables measuring a little[100] over three feet across, and six of a rather smaller[110] size. Yours respectfully, (113)

Facility Practice 9 (see p. 136 for Key)

(a) 

(b) 

(c) 

(d) 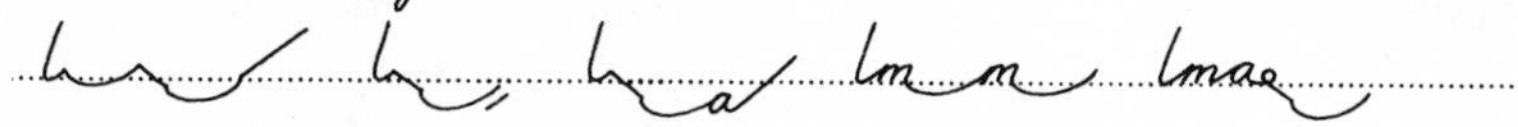

Vocabulary drill

burn
burned
burning
burns
burnt
business
businesses
businesslike
businessman
but
buy
by
bye
buying
buys
buyer
buyers
call
called
calling
calls
caller

Drill based on Dictation Passage 10

falling
particular
woman
balanced
friends
relations
without
modern
easier
wonderful
tradesmen

frequently	it must be
records	there was
equally	on which
against	would not
heart	I knew
with the	that is*
it was	for me
it was not	
so much	

***Note:** .... = *that is*, whereas .... = *this is*.

Compare .... = *without* and .... = *with the*.

The sign for *the* is always written with the slope ..../..... . It is therefore kept quite distinct from the downstroke T ....⟍...., and the figure ..1.... .

Dictation Passage 10 (see p. 111 for PitmanScript)

(The House)

Falling in love with that particular house was like falling[10] in love with the wrong woman – at least, the wrong[20] woman in the eyes of all one's more balanced friends[30] and relations. Every consideration of common sense was against the[40] house. It was old and without any of the little[50] modern touches that make living so much easier; it was[60] not even clean, and I would have to spend much[70] of my small store of money in doing it up.[80] Its situation was wonderful, except for the fact, it must[90] be added, that it was miles from a town of[100] any kind, that there was no made-up road leading[110] to it, and that tradesmen were not likely to be[120] over-willing to deliver goods frequently enough to meet simple[130] general requirements. Even the weather there was known to be[140] bad, its records showing up very poorly against many other[150] equally beautiful places – for beautiful it was, and that was[160] something on which few people would not agree.

All these[170] things were against the place, I knew, and that is[180] why I told myself on that lovely June evening when[190] I first saw the house that it was not for[200] me. It is true that I was, in a careless[210] kind of way, keeping my eye open for a likely[220] house, but I was careless about it because, after all,[230] I already had a house, which was more than a[240] number of people had at that time, and it was[250] a modern house and quite satisfactory in most respects. But[260] there was something about that old house, seen in the[270] clear light of an early June evening, that reached out[280] and touched my heart. There was a special quality about[290] it which seemed to answer to some special quality in[300] me. Perhaps we were both a little off balance, not[310] made for the world of common sense and hard facts. (320)

This passage is continued in Dictation Passage 11.

Facility Practice 10 (see p. 136 for Key)

(a)
(b)
(c)
(d)
(e)

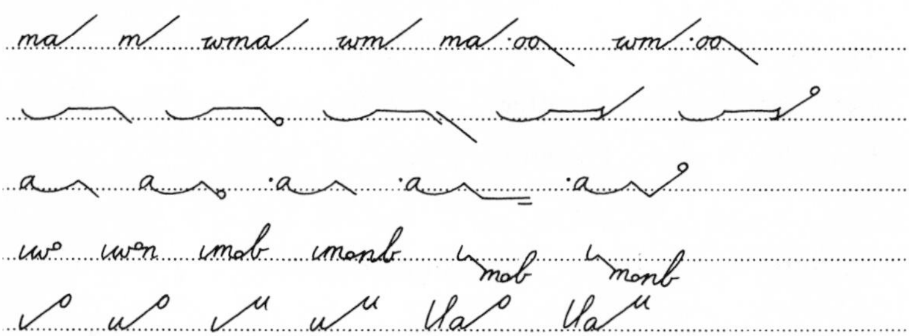

Spelling: Note the repeated letters which are underlined in the following words: ambassador, dissimilar, professor, aggressor, caterpillar, predecessor.

As pointed out earlier, letters which are repeated in longhand spelling but which represent only *one* sound are not repeated in PitmanScript:

In *predecessor*, the first circle represents the *c* and the second circle represents the two *s*'s.

Vocabulary drill

came	**care**
can	cared
cannot	caring
capital	cares
capitals	careful
capitalist	carefully
capitalists	carefulness
car	careless
cars	carelessly
	carelessness

Drill based on Dictation Passage 11

south	existence
west	stored
north	afterwards
east	to take away
limitless	I must have been
although	I did not
knowledge	it is possible

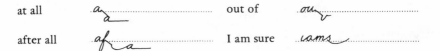

at all		out of	
after all		I am sure	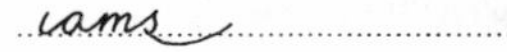

Note: Good links are those which join the forms for words which naturally run together in speech, such as: *out of, at all, it is possible.*

Dictation Passage 11 (see p. 112 for PitmanScript)

(The House, continued)

The house had been built on a small point of[10] land with water on three sides of it. To the[20] south there was a river running into the sea, and[30] to the west and north was the sea itself, not[40] the great open sea, limitless and troubled, but a small[50] arm of the sea with enough movement of the water[60] to add interest but not enough to take away from[70] the general feeling of peace which seemed so much a[80] part of the whole place. I must have been lost[90] then, although I did not know it. It was indeed[100] two years later that I finally bought the house. During[110] those two years I hardly thought of the house at[120] all. It is possible that the knowledge of its existence[130] and all that it might mean to me was stored[140] away in the back of my mind and that I[150] played about with the idea of buying the place. If[160] so, I knew nothing of these deeper thoughts of mine.[170] All I know for certain is that on a June[180] morning two years afterwards I got out of bed with[190] my mind already made up for me. I had not[200] been thinking about the house, of that I am sure,[210] but as I dressed I knew that I was taking[220] the first train north and that I was going to[230] buy that house and live in it, and be happy[240] in it.

And I did buy it and live in[250] it, but the happiness which I found in it had[260] after all nothing to do with the house itself. (269)

Facility Practice 11 (see p. 136 for Key)

(a) 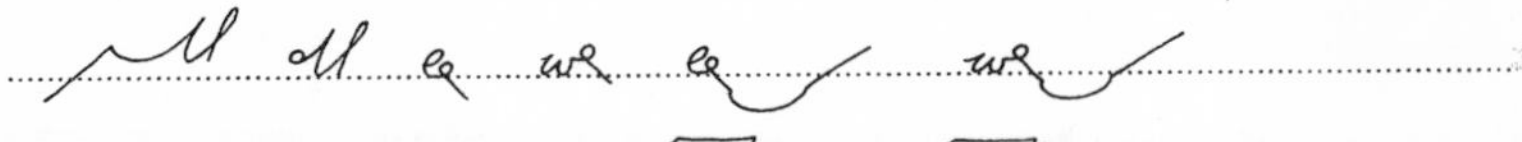

(b) 

(c) 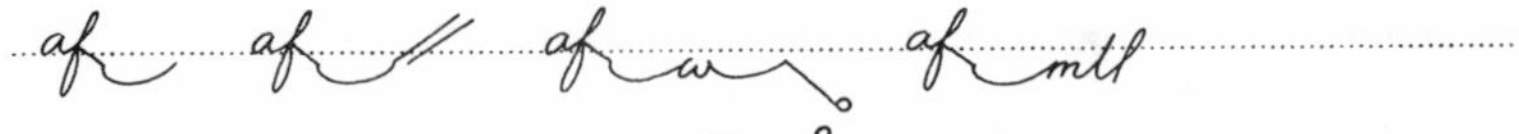

(d) 

(e) 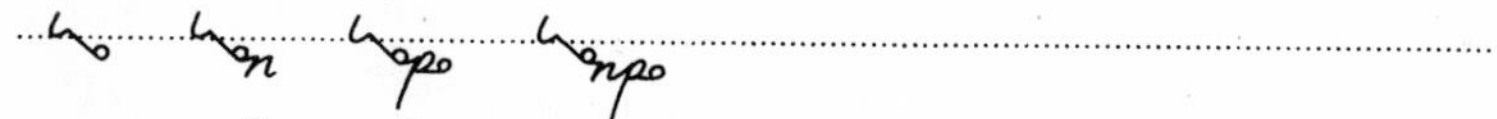

(f) 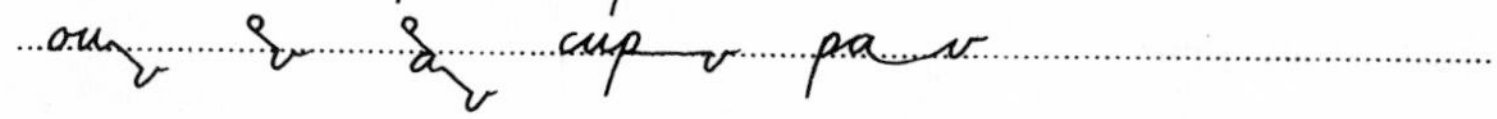

Note in (f) the addition of a final *v* to represent the word *of*. Links of this kind are very easy to write and read back.

Vocabulary drill

carry	**chief**
case	**child**
cause	**children**
certain	
certainly	**city**
certainty	citizen
change	**clean**
changeless	cleaner
character	cleanest
characteristic	**clear**
charge	clearly
cheap	clearer
cheaper	**coal**
cheapest	coalfield
cheaply	coalmine
check	**coarse** / **course**
cheque	**cold**

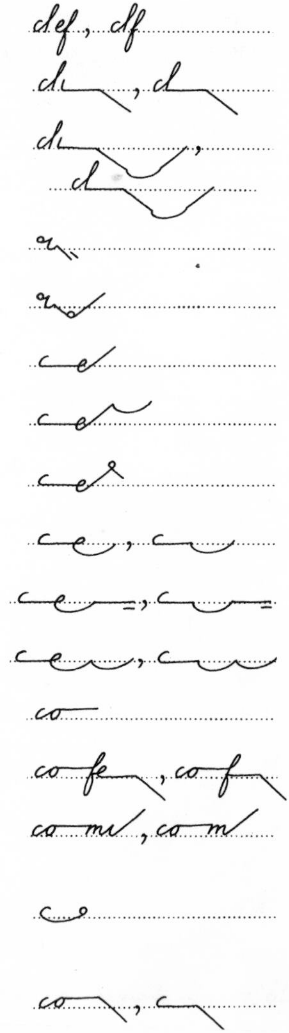

The common suffixes *-s*, *-ed* and *-ing* are not included in this drill or following drills, as the writer has now had plenty of practice in adding them.

Drill based on Dictation Passage 12

usual
yesterday
newspapers
director
expressing
engineer
members
responsible
principal
willingness

matter of fact
leading part
yesterday afternoon
this was
he would
he could
at present

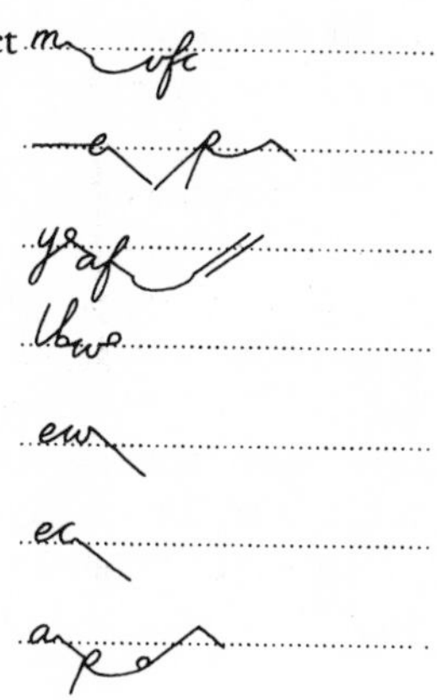

Dictation Passage 12 (see p. 113 for PitmanScript)

(Presentation of an Oil Painting)

A pleasing little event broke the usual matter of fact[10] course of a company meeting yesterday afternoon when an oil[20] painting of himself was given to Mr H E Fell,[30] who for 25 years has been a member of[40] the board of General Newspapers. A second picture in oils[50] will, when ready, be put in the board room of[60] the company.

Mr Wells, director, in handing over the painting,[70] said that for almost 70 years Mr Fell and his[80] father had played a leading part in the direction of[90] the company, and this was certainly a record in which[100] any family might take considerable pleasure.

In expressing his deep[110] thanks to the board for their thoughtful action, Mr Fell[120] said that shortly after he first took his place on[130] the board of the company he had given up his[140] own business as an engineer and since that time had[150] given all his time and work to the interests of[160] the company. He was deeply touched by the kindness of[170] the members of the board, and he would, of course,[180] continue to do everything he could in the best interests[190] of General Newspapers.

Mr Fell then went on to speak[200] of the position of the company and stated that companies[210] responsible for publishing newspapers were at present having to face[220] many difficulties, and not the least of these was the[230] stopping of the usual supplies of paper. When these supplies[240] were cut off the principal newspapers of the country had[250] got together and had formed a new supply company. They[260] all put capital into the new company and bought paper[270] from a different part of the world, and even bought[280] ships to bring in that paper. This action on the[290] part of different newspapers, holding different views, was a good[300] example of what willingness and organization can do.

After the[310] meeting members took the opportunity to view the oil painting,[320] and all agreed that it was a work of art[330] of very high quality. (334)

Facility Practice 12 (see p. 137 for Key)

(a) 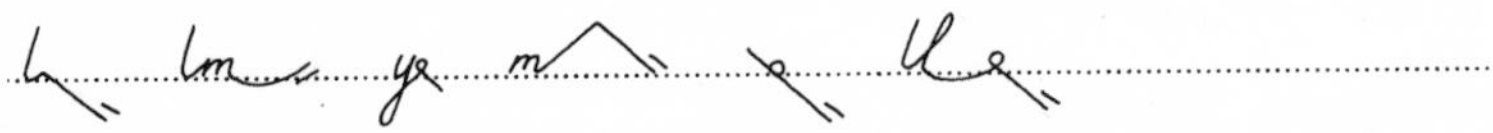

(b) 

(c) 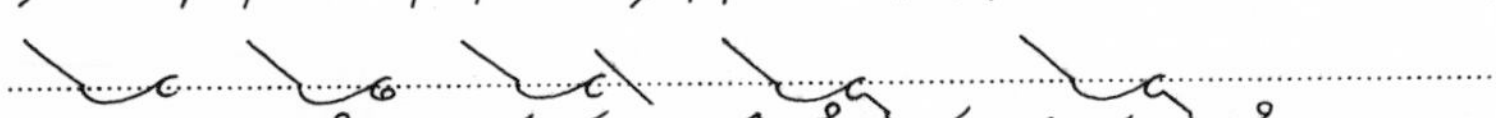

(d) 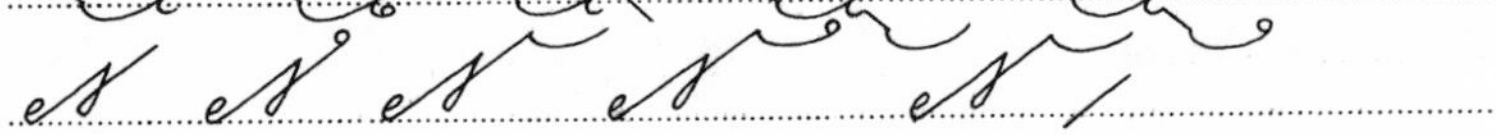

(e) 

(f) 

Vocabulary drill

colour

colourful

come

comfort

comfortable

commit

commitment

committee

common

company

competition

complete

completion

condition

conditional

connect

connexion

consider

consideration

considerable

continue

continuance

continuous

control

copy

cost

Drill based on Dictation Passage 13

outcome

strong

indeed

third

within

outlets

property

monthly

service

government

resulting	in the first place
upon the	in the second place
work of	rate of interest
to be able to	from us
been able to	to us
report and accounts	with us
we need have	course of events
past year	there have been

Dictation Passage 13 (see p. 114 for PitmanScript)

(Statement regarding the position of a company)

The many difficulties which are the necessary outcome of the[10] past will continue, and the weight of changing conditions is[20] likely to have an ever-increasing effect upon the work[30] of a company such as this, whose chief interest is[40] in connexion with the building trade. It is, therefore, highly[50] satisfactory to me to be able to state that not[60] only has your company been able to face up to[70] these difficult conditions but that the accounts for the year[80] show that we are in a very strong position indeed.[90] As you know, this is the third largest company of[100] its kind in the country and, judging from the report[110] and accounts now before you, we need have no immediate[120] fear for the safety of our leading position.

It will[130] be within the knowledge of most of you here that[140] certain important changes have been announced during the past year.[150] The directors found it necessary in the first place to[160] limit the sums of money placed in their hands by[170] the public for safe keeping, and in the second place[180] they recently announced a fall in the rate of interest[190] payable on such money. I think I should say a[200] few words to you now regarding the reasons which influenced[210] the directors to take these steps. The recent fall in[220] the building of new houses has taken from us one[230] of our largest outlets for the use of our money.[240] Indeed, it is the payment of sums of money to[250] would-be house owners which is the chief object of[260] a company such as ours. We are now left with[270] large sums of money coming to us in the form[280] of monthly payments and this money must for the most[290] part go into the service of the government in one[300] way or another. This means a lower rate of interest,[310] with a resulting fall in the income of the company.[320] It says much for the strong position which we hold[330] in the minds of the public that there have been[340] signs of an increased desire to place money with us,[350] and it may be necessary for us to control this[360] movement. Some check has to be found and this will[370] probably be to change the rate of interest payable on[380] new money received by us. In addition, the directors are[390] taking the further course of limiting the amount of money[400] which can be placed with us. (406)

Facility Practice 13 (see p. 137 for Key)

(a)
(b)
(c)
(d)
(e)

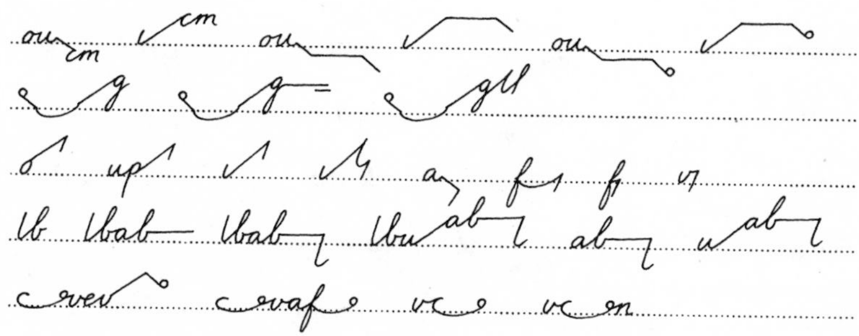

Vocabulary drill

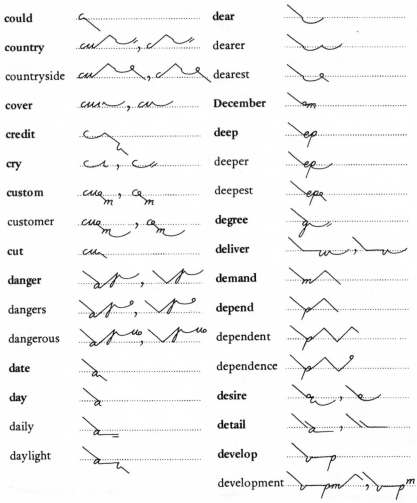

could
country
countryside
cover
credit
cry
custom
customer
cut
danger
dangers
dangerous
date
day
daily
daylight

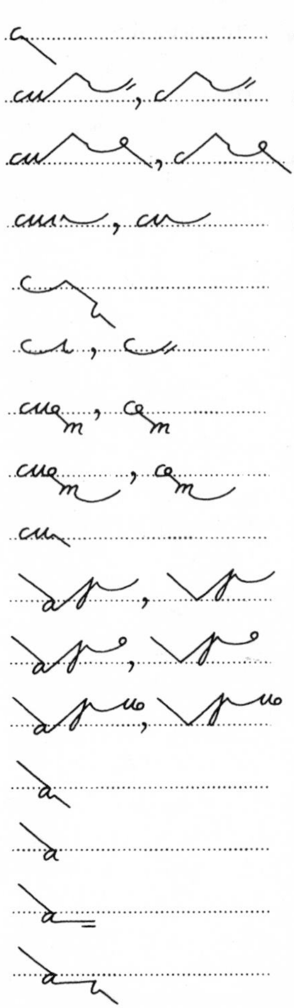

dear
dearer
dearest
December
deep
deeper
deepest
degree
deliver
demand
depend
dependent
dependence
desire
detail
develop
development

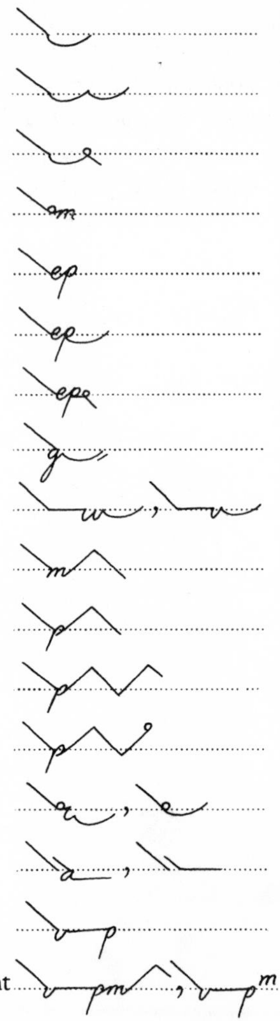

Drill based on Dictation Passage 14

horse
watch

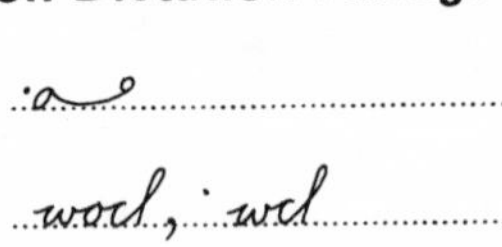

happen
remember

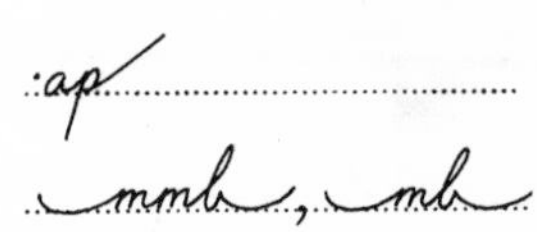

memories	mm ɹ, im ɹ	there had been	ll a b
pulling	p /	there would be	ll w b
another	a ull, a ll	they would	ll aw
warm	wa m, w m	there were	ll w
pleasure	p j	he was	ews
summer	sum, sm	you can have a	uc ava
perhaps	p apo	I would like	iw lk
neither	/ll, /l	in the world	i w
young	yu g, y g	once more	w sm
sweet	swe		

Dictation Passage 14 (see p. 115 for PitmanScript)

The old horse was holding his head up so that[10] he could see over the wires and watch the road.[20] It seemed to the horse that he had spent all[30] the days of all his life doing this same thing[40] in this same field, waiting for something to happen. But[50] there had been other and better days, because he could[60] still remember events in the past. Yes, the old broken[70]-down horse had his memories, memories of days spent pulling[80] heavy weights along long, long roads. Sometimes there would be[90] another horse at his side, and they would pull together.[100] Sometimes they would stop for water by the road-side,[110] and how good that water had been, so clean and[120] so cold, quite different from the half-warm water he[130] had to drink in this field. Then there were memories[140] of days spent working on a farm. Those were good[150] days, very good. He had been a great and strong[160] and healthy animal, and there was pleasure in the work,[170] hard though it had been at times. The only trouble[180] had been the flies. Oh, those flies on those warm[190] summer days! There were not so many flies in this[200] field, and perhaps that was a good thing. But if[210] there were no flies, neither was there much that was[220] good. Day after day he spent, waiting for something to[230] happen, but nothing ever did happen.

A long time ago[240] a number of young men used to stand about in[250] the road. They would come in the evenings and talk,[260] and they often said the place was a backwater. "We[270] shall never get on if we stop in this backwater,"[280] they used to say. There was one young man he[290] particularly liked, for he was certain to bring something sweet[300] and give it to the old horse, but the young[310] men did not come now. No one came. When he[320] had been led into this field his master had said:[330] "Now you can have a long rest, old boy, and[340] believe me that is just what I would like to[350] do." But as the old horse remembered this and other[360] things he continued to stand and watch the road, and[370] the thing he was waiting for was the day when[380] someone would come along and take him away, and put[390] him to useful work once more. (396)

Facility Practice 14 (see p. 137 for Key)

(a)
(b)
(c)
(d)

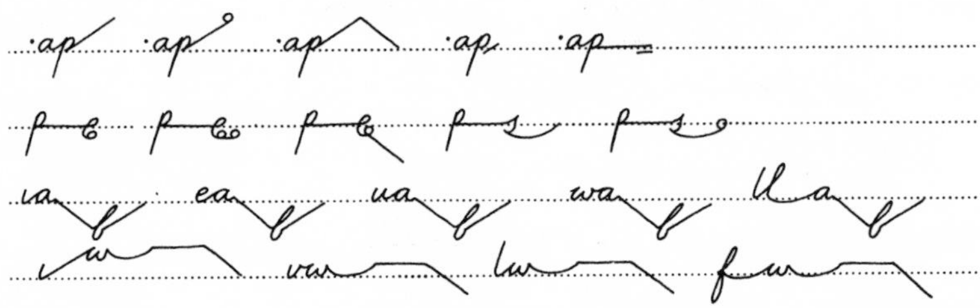

Vocabulary drill

die
died
differ
difference
different
difficult
difficulty
direct
direction
discover
distance
distant
distribute
distribution
division
divisional

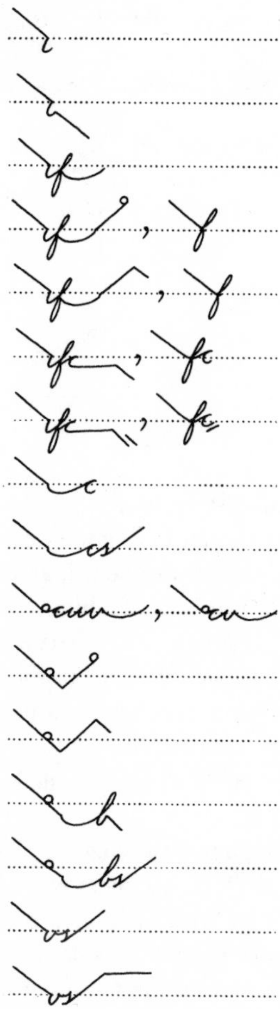

do
doing
does
done
did
door
doubt
doubtful
down
dress
dressmaker
drink
drank
drunk
drive
driven
drove
during

Drill based on Dictation Passage 15

wishes	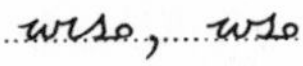	we wish	
health		year by year	
success	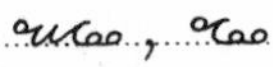	side by side	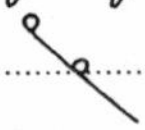
controlling	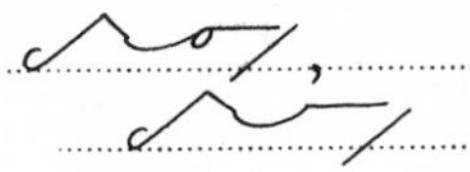	it would not be	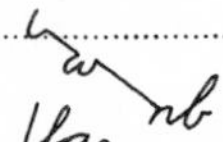
		to face the	
whether			
wisely	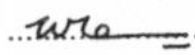		

Dictation Passage 15 (see p. 117 for PitmanScript)

I know that you will all wish me to offer[10] to Mr R T Weeks our very deep wishes for[20] his happiness and for his quick return to good health.[30] After many years of service, Mr Weeks has now left[40] our board, and to say that we thank him for[50] his past services is to say too little. To him,[60] and perhaps only to him, do we really owe our[70] great success as an oil undertaking. For more than thirty[80] years he has been the controlling influence in the building[90] up of this company, and if we wish to see[100] whether he has done well or otherwise we have only[110] to look at our past records. Year by year we[120] have gone forward, and there can be no doubt at[130] all that we shall in the future greatly miss his[140] wise help and judgment.

I feel myself to be a[150] very poor person to be taking his place on the[160] board. I cannot hope to be as wise and as[170] far-seeing as was my chief, for men are not[180] all like one another, and Mr Weeks had greatness in[190] him. It would not be possible, however, to work side[200] by side with him, year in and year out, without[210] learning much, and I think I can say with truth[220] that I have indeed learned a great amount during those[230] years which will help me to act wisely in the[240] interests of the company in the difficult years through which[250] we are now passing. When I do less well than[260] you might have hoped, I trust you will look kindly[270] upon me, knowing that there is a limit to my[280] powers; and when I do better than might have been[290] expected I trust that you will remember my old chief,[300] as I shall, and give him credit for teaching me[310] well.

The records of our past history stand clear for[320] all to see. The future is not clear to any[330] of us. We can plan and we can try to[340] plan well, so that when better times come we shall[350] be ready to act in this or that way, according[360] to the turn of events. Therefore, I ask you now[370] to spend some little time this afternoon in a consideration[380] of possible future plans, with special consideration to future means[390] of shipment, the future buying of the best possible plant[400] for our special purposes, and such other matters as are[410] of the deepest interest to us. It is of the[420] highest importance that we have clear-cut plans ready to[430] put into operation at the moment when conditions show themselves[440] to be satisfactory. (443)

Facility Practice 15 (see p. 137 for Key)

(a)
(b)
(c)
(d)

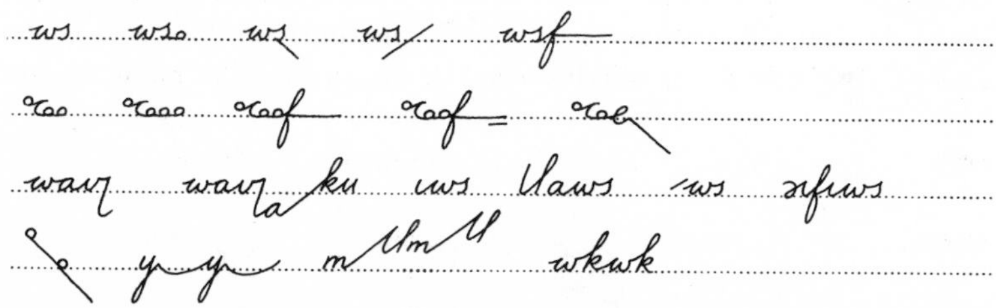

Spelling: Here are some tricky words so far as spelling is concerned: *cynicism*, *criticism*, *mysticism*, *syllogism*, *schism*. The forms for these words are:

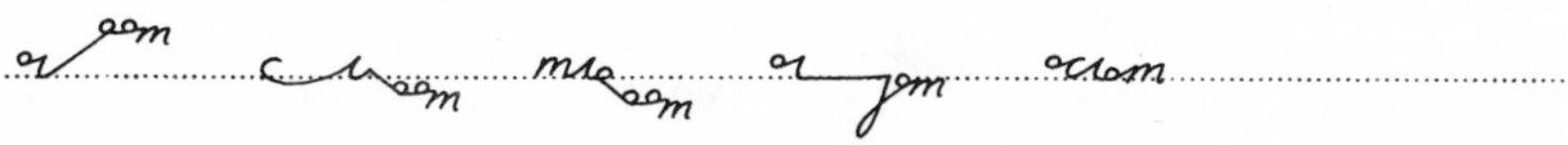

It will be noted that whether the sound of *s* is spelt with a *c* or an *s* the small circle is used to represent it; and also that whether the vowel sound *i* is spelt with an *i* or a *y* it is always represented by .

This concludes Unit 1, in which all the dictation passages use only the 700 most common words or their derivatives.

Unit 2
Dictation practice based on the 2000 most common words

Vocabulary drill

Although the dictation material covers the 2000 most common words, the full list of the 700 will continue to be given in the course of this book. Only unusual derivative forms will, however, be shown from this point onwards.

each
early
earth
ease
east
education
effect
either
electric
employ
end
engine
English
enough
equal
even
event
ever
example
except
exchange
exist
expect
experience
expert
express

eye	ı	**fall**	fa
face	fao	**family**	fam, fm
fact	fac		

Drill based on Dictation Passages 16(a) and 16(b)

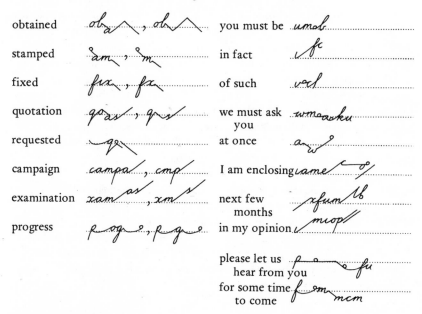

obtained	ob, ob	you must be	umob
stamped	am, m	in fact	ıfc
fixed	fix, fx	of such	vocl
quotation	qoas, q	we must ask you	wmoaoku
requested	q	at once	aw
campaign	campa, cmp	I am enclosing	ıame
examination	xamas, xm	next few months	xfum
progress	pog, pg	in my opinion	ımıop
		please let us hear from you	fu
		for some time to come	fsm mcm

Dictation Passage 16(a) (see p. 118 for PitmanScript)

Dear Mr Johnson, Our attention has this week been called[10] to the fact that you are quoting special prices to[20] your customers for goods obtained from us and stamped with[30] our trade mark. We know that you must be acquainted[40] with our rule that all goods which bear this stamp[50] must be sold at the prices fixed by us. All[60] our customers, without exception, sign an agreement with us not[70] to sell below the fixed prices, and we have here,[80] in fact, a copy of such an agreement between you[90] and us. This rule is necessary if we are to[100] prevent price cutting, which has caused so much difficulty and[110] trouble in the trade in the past. We must ask[120] you to take any special quotation for our goods from[130] your list at once, as it will otherwise be impossible[140] for us to supply you with any lines which bear[150] our stamp. Please let us hear from you regarding this[160] point within the next three days. Yours truly, (168)

Dictation Passage 16(b) (see p. 119 for PitmanScript)

As requested, I am enclosing an account of the market[10] in your goods for the past quarter. I have in[20] this case gone into figures, etc, in more detail than[30] usual, as I feel that exact information on certain points[40] will help you to decide on what lines to run[50] your campaign during the next few months. As you will[60] see, the market was inclined to be very quiet for[70] the first four weeks of the quarter, but at the[80] beginning of February there was a quick improvement over the[90] whole country, and prices generally increased. There has, on the[100] whole, been a better market in the north than in[110] the south, and I have to admit that I find[120] it a little difficult to account for this. I am,[130] however, making a close examination of the figures in an[140] attempt to arrive at the reason for the difference.

The[150] present quarter has opened well, and so far the market[160] from your point of view is a quite satisfactory one.[170] In my opinion you should be well satisfied with the[180] progress you are making. With things as they are, it[190] does not seem to me that you will require to[200] spend a great deal of money on your next campaign.[210] I believe that you are able to hold the ground[220] already won, and even to win more ground, without very[230] much expense for some time to come. (237)

Facility Practice 16 (see p. 138 for Key)

(a) (b) (c) (d)

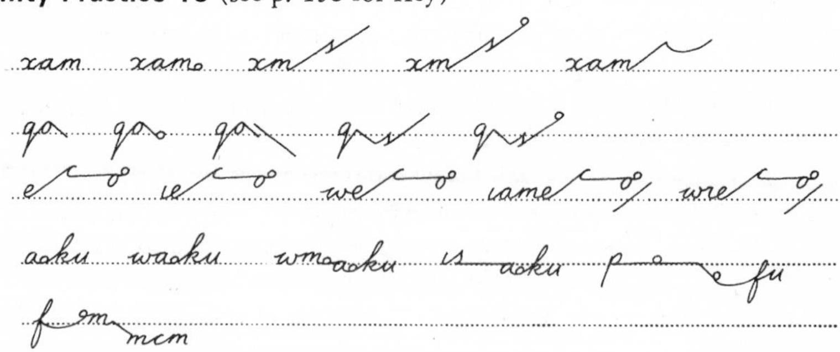

Special Signs: Here are twenty-four Special Signs – just as a reminder that they are time-savers and should be used when taking notes:

t = the	*d* = do	*ye* = yesterday
o = is	*t* = to/too	*f* = for/fore
:o = his	*n* = not	*tt* = there/their
b = these	*p* = put	*s* = shall
w = we	*tt* = that	*w* = will
m = me	*tb* = this	*g* = thing
v = of	*cl* = which	*k* = think
f = from	*wtt* = with	*a^k* = thank

Vocabulary drill

far		food	
farm		foot	
father		for	
fear		force	
February		form	
feel		forward	
few		free	
field		frequent	
figure		Friday	
final		friend	
find		from	
fire		front	
first		full	
fish		further	
fly		future	
follow		general	

Drill based on Dictation Passage 17

confidence		securing	
definite		college	

decide

correspondence

extremely

towards

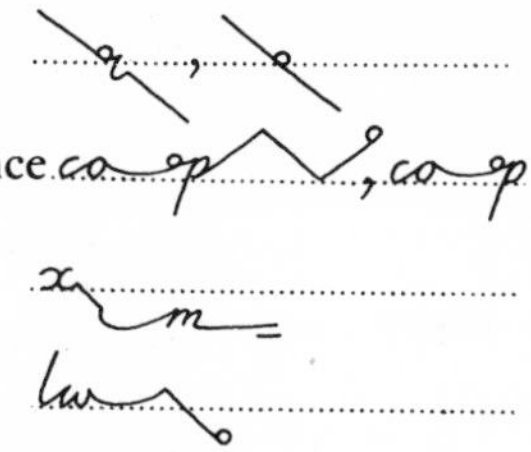

to meet

have you taken

to make the

this can be

in the first place

Dictation Passage 17 (see p. 119 for PitmanScript)

Are you wondering what the future will hold for you?[10] Can you face it with confidence? Are you expecting to[20] meet with success, and have you taken any definite step[30] towards securing success? If you are not content merely to[40] accept whatever happens to come along, if you intend to[50] make the very best of your own ability, this college[60] can help you. We can help you in the first[70] place by telling you what possibility there is of your[80] meeting with success in the different kinds of business open[90] to you. Afterwards we can help you by giving you[100] the training necessary for any examinations connected with the particular[110] field of business which you may decide to enter. By[120] means of our correspondence course, you can work through a[130] carefully planned and extremely interesting course of study bearing directly[140] upon your special needs. This can be done in the[150] quiet of your own home, and under my personal direction.[160] Don't delay. Fill in the attached card, and return it[170] to the college today. By so doing, you will be[180] taking your first step forward toward future success. (188)

Note:  = *don't*, to distinguish it from dn = *do not.*

Facility Practice 17 (see p. 138 for Key)

(a)
(b)
(c)
(d)
(e)

Vocabulary drill

gentlemen	hard
get	has
girl	have
give	he
go	head
gold	health
good	hear / here
govern	heart
great	heat
ground	heavy
grow	help
had	her
half	high
hand	him
happen	his
happy	history

Drill based on Dictation Passage 18

communication	conversation
telephone	community

available	ava-b, av-b
conference	cf
complaint	cmp-a, cmp
consequently	cq
extent	x

referring to your communication of	flu cm cs
have pleasure	avp-s
I regret the	ugy
I am confident	iamcf
as soon as possible	aspo
in view of a	vuva
in connection with	ccwll

Note: The syllable *con-* is written c, and the syllable *com-* is written cm. Also note that *-sion* is s and *-asion* is generally as, although experienced writers may safely omit the a.

Dictation Passage 18 (see p. 120 for PitmanScript)

Dear Sir, Referring to your communication of 2nd December and[10] to our telephone conversation this morning, I now have pleasure[20] in forwarding to you some details of the Third Annual[30] Trade Convention, to be held in the New Community Hall[40] during the month of January. I regret that I am[50] not in a position to send you today a plan[60] of the floor space available, as the members of the[70] committee are still in conference regarding one or two important[80] points. I am confident, however, that you will have no[90] difficulty in securing for your firm space not only sufficient[100] in size but, in addition, attractive in location.

In view[110] of a complaint made last year that the volume of[120] advertising in connection with the convention was not sufficient to[130] draw the public in large numbers, it has been decided[140] this year to increase the amount to be spent in[150] this way. We are consequently hoping for excellent results this[160] year. You can depend upon my forwarding the final details[170] to you as soon as possible, and in the meantime[180] perhaps you will let me know exactly what space you[190] would like to have. I will do my best to[200] secure it for you. Yours truly, (206)

Facility Practice 18 (see p. 138 for Key)

(a) 

(b) 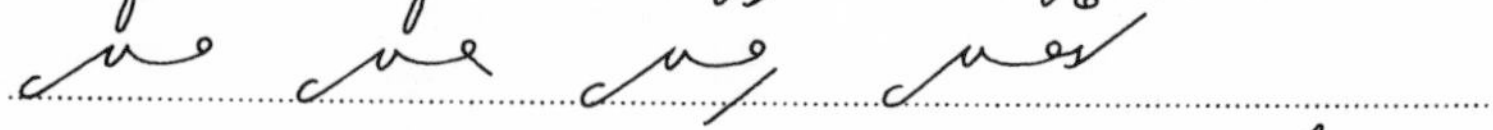

(c) 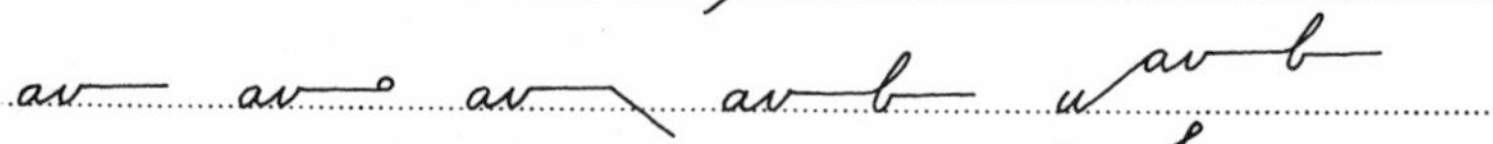

(d) 

(e) 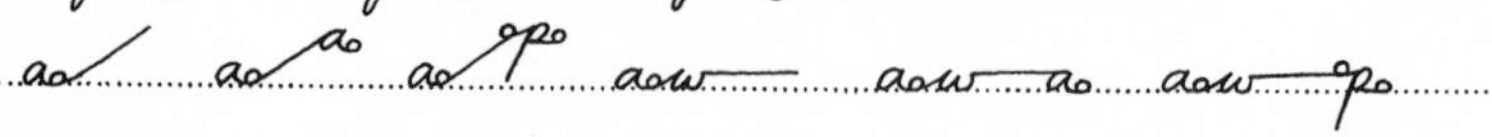

Spelling: *aversion, expansion, extension, intercession, succession, admiration, defection, vocation, musician, fashion.* There are five different ways of spelling the sound of *shun* in these words: *-sion, -ssion, -tion, -cian, -shion.* In all cases the PitmanScript form is 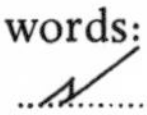, as:

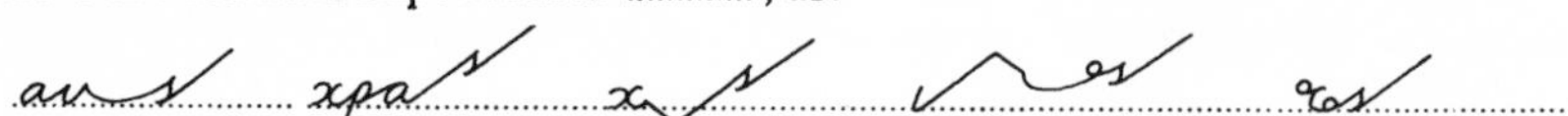

If the termination is *s*-vowel-*shun*, the PitmanScript form is . If it is particularly desired to show the vowel, it may be inserted – as:

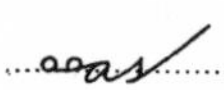 = *cessation,* 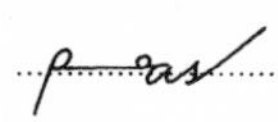 = *pulsation.*

For the termination *-uation* it is generally sufficient to write 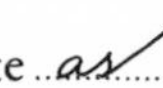 :

 = *situation,*  = *punctuation.* Compare:  = *station,*  = situation. Here again, however, the  may be omitted in familiar words:  = *situation.*

Vocabulary drill

hold	in
hole	increase
home	indeed
hope	industry
horse	influence
hour	inform
house	instruction
how	insurance
however	interest
I	iron
idea	is
if	issue
immediate	it
important	January
impossible	judge
improve	July

Drill based on Dictation Passages 19(a) and 19(b)

accordance	glass
parcel	flowers

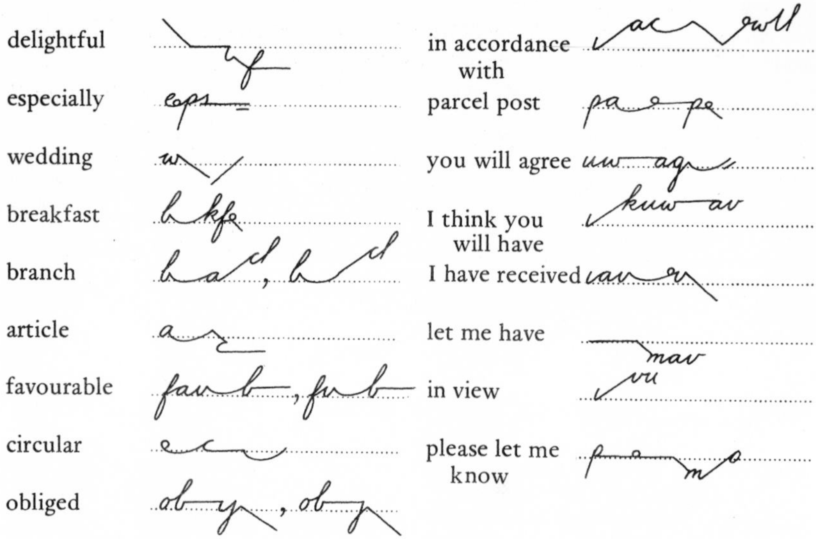

branch		I have received	
article		let me have	
favourable		in view	
circular		please let me know	
obliged

Remember that links are intended to save time in writing by avoiding lifts of the pen. Words may be written separately if preferred.

Dictation Passage 19(a) (see p. 121 for PitmanScript)

Dear Sir, In accordance with your wishes, I have forwarded[10] to you today by parcel post samples of our new[20] glass flowers and small glass trees. I am sure you[30] will agree that these are delightful in their clear beauty,[40] and that they are especially suitable for table use at[50] big affairs, such as a dinner party or a wedding[60] breakfast, or at any time when it is necessary to[70] have flowers on the table for several hours. Please note[80] that the colour in which we supply these flowers can[90] be changed at any time. To do this all that[100] is necessary is to replace the small light at the[110] foot of each branch with a light of a different[120] colour.

I think you will have little trouble in bringing[130] this beautiful new article to the favourable notice of your[140] customers. Yours respectfully, (143)

Dictation Passage 19(b) (see p. 121 for PitmanScript)

Dear Sir, I have received your circular today with description[10] and prices of the different grades of leather which you[20] supply for making cases and other goods. I shall be[30] glad if you will permit me to accept your offer[40] of free samples of your leather, as I should like[50] to give your firm a trial.

This is a retail[60] store, and my principal business is the supply of leather[70] cases to suit the personal wishes of customers. I do[80] an extremely large business in this way, and if any[90] of your grades of leather are suitable for my purpose,[100] I can promise you plenty of valuable business. In view[110] of this, may I ask you to state the most[120] favourable terms on which you could let me have monthly[130] supplies of leather. Please let me know your days of[140] delivery, and when I may expect to receive samples. Yours[150] truly, (151)

Facility Practice 19 (see p. 138 for Key)

(a)
(b)
(c)
(d)
(e)
(f)

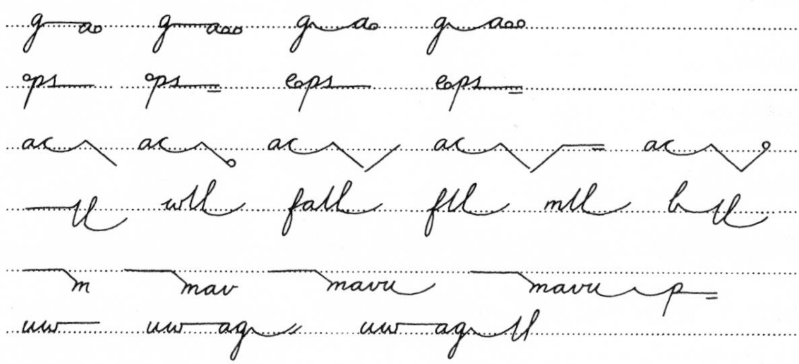

Vocabulary drill

June	least
just	leave
keep	left
kind	less
king	let
know	letter
knowledge	life
labour	light
land	like
language	limit
large	line
last	list
late	little
law	live
lead	long
learn	look

Drill based on Dictation Passage 20

occasion	union*
insurance	operation

premium		annual meeting of the	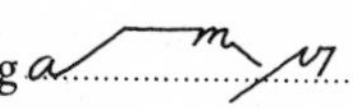
somewhat	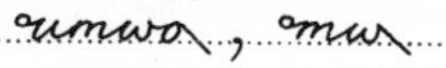	3 million dollars†	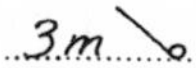
dollars†		our own	
circumstances		at home	
realize	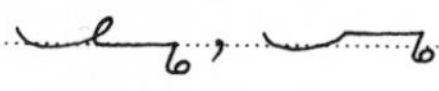		
commercial			
settled			

Note: Compare the link  = *at home*, with  = *atom* in which the second vowel carries no stress and may be omitted.

* If it is ever felt necessary to distinguish between *union* and *onion*, the dot may be placed over the u̇ to show that the diphthong is intended. Normally, however, such distinction is quite unnecessary.

† When following a figure,  is adequate for *dollars*.

Dictation Passage 20 (see p. 122 for PitmanScript)

On the occasion of the recent annual meeting of the[10] American Insurance Union the chairman said: The results of the[20] operation of our Union for the past twelve months may[30] be taken as showing that every section of our business[40] has obtained some benefit from the general improvement in world[50] conditions. Our fire premium was somewhat lower than that of[60] the previous financial year, but it is worthy of note[70] that none of this loss occurred in our valuable home[80] market.

Our own loss experience was extremely favourable, and the[90] fire department shows a profit for the twelve months of[100] over three million dollars. Considering all the circumstances, I think[110] this may be considered a very satisfactory result.

The premium[120] in our general department is also a little lower than[130] it has been for the previous twelve months. The home[140] section of the account in this case shows a somewhat[150] lower result. Both at home and throughout the world results[160] have not been satisfactory. This is an experience in which[170] we are not by any means alone. Everyone with an[180] understanding of present-day conditions must realize that our needs[190] today are the needs of the whole world – goodwill, more[200] commercial trade between country and country, and a settled exchange[210] rate. (211)

Facility Practice 20 (see p. 139 for Key)

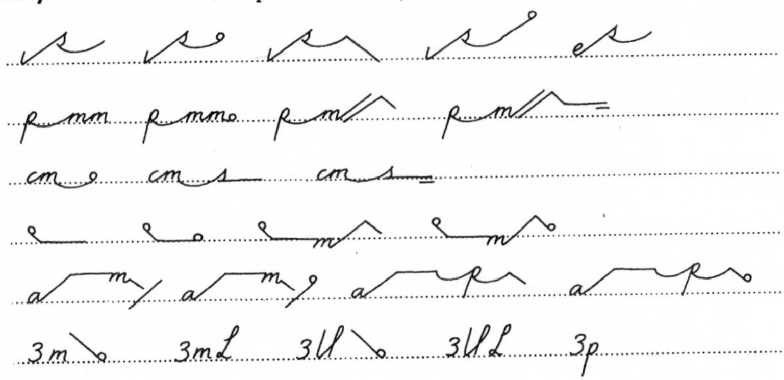

(a)

(b)

(c)

(d)

(e)

(f)

Vocabulary drill

loss
love
low
machine
made / maid
make
man
manufacture
many
march
mark
market
marry
mass
master
matter

may
me
meal
mean
measure
meat / meet
member
memory
mere
method
might
mile
milk
million
mind
mine

Drill based on Dictation Passage 21

lake
intended

district
human

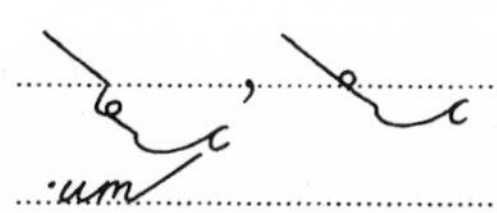

actually
indicated
outfit
wild
mountains
undoubtedly
ordinary
centre

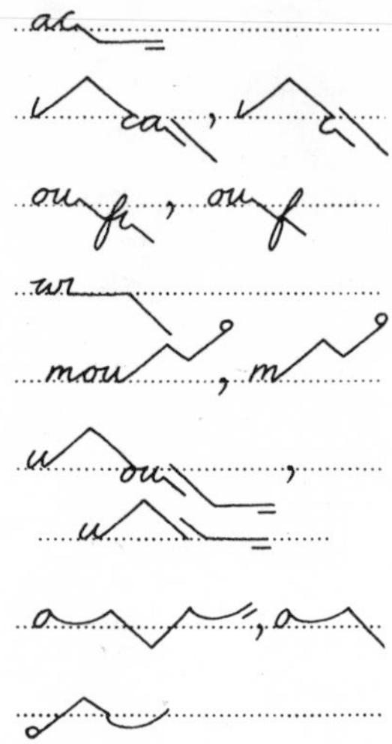

I had been
I went
I saw
I did not
he told me
I learned

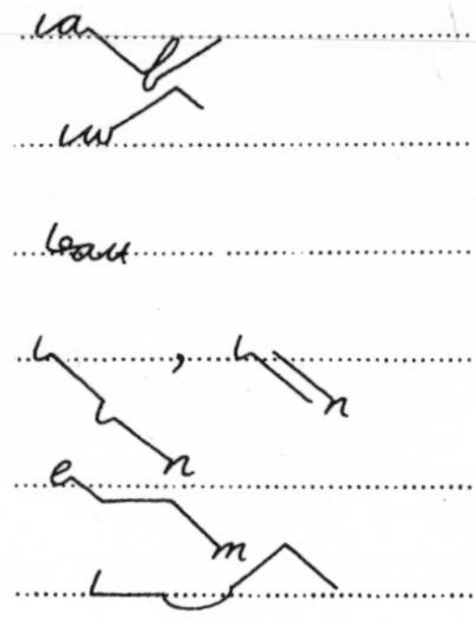

Dictation Passage 21 (see p. 123 for PitmanScript)

After some days I reached the lake where I intended[10] to camp, my object being to study the wild life[20] of the district. I had been told that I was[30] mad to attempt to stay long in such a place,[40] as no human being had been there for years. I[50] was also assured that the lake was so deep that[60] although a party of men had once tried to sound[70] it the attempt had failed.

I was naturally surprised, therefore,[80] on the third day of my stay to come upon[90] a rough little building standing alone in the middle of[100] a field, about a quarter of a mile from the[110] water. From the sounds I heard, I knew that somebody[120] was actually living there, and as I went through the[130] mud towards the building I saw an old man at[140] the door.

In some way which at the time I[150] did not understand he seemed to fit in naturally with[160] the country around him. He held out his hand, and[170] indicated that I was at liberty to enter his strange[180] little outfit. We quickly became friends, and he told me[190] of his life in this wild place, and said that[200] he desired to live alone as he felt that life[210] was too short and too valuable to be spent in[220] the rush of the modern world. He lived here summer[230] and winter, and had to depend entirely upon himself for[240] support.

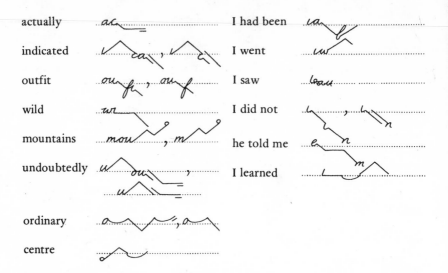

His needs were simple and few, and for friends[250] he had his books. From him I learned much of[260] interest to me in my study, as he had a[270] wonderful knowledge of the wild life of the lake and[280] the mountains. He told me also that he had himself[290] been able to sound every foot of the lake. It[300] was undoubtedly a strange life for a man to lead,[310] but it seemed to give him perfect happiness and to[320] satisfy the needs of his spirit. I am quite sure[330] that when I left him to return to the ordinary[340] life of the city, with its many interests, he was[350] very much pleased to be alone once again, the centre[360] of his own little world. (365)

Facility Practice 21 (see p. 139 for Key)

(a)
(b)
(c)
(d)
(e)
(f)

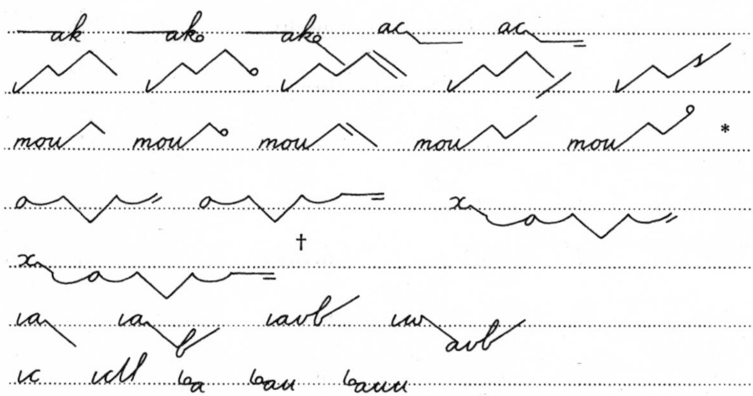

*The ou would be omitted when the meaning is obvious.

† The form 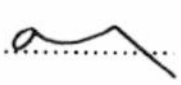 may be used when the context makes the meaning clear.

Vocabulary drill

minute		my	
miss		name	
modern		nation	
moment		nature	
Monday		near	
money		necessary	
month		need	
more		neither	
morning		never	
most		new	
mother		next	
motor		night	
move		nor	
Mr		north	
much		not	
must		note	

Drill based on Dictation Passages 22(a) and (b)

organization		factory	
publication		originally	

investigation
manager
department
invoice

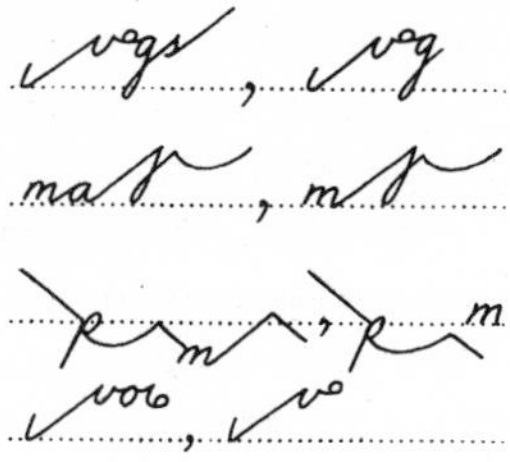

thank you for your
of yesterday
I hope you will do
as soon as
I shall be obliged
let me know
first week
last week
as we have said

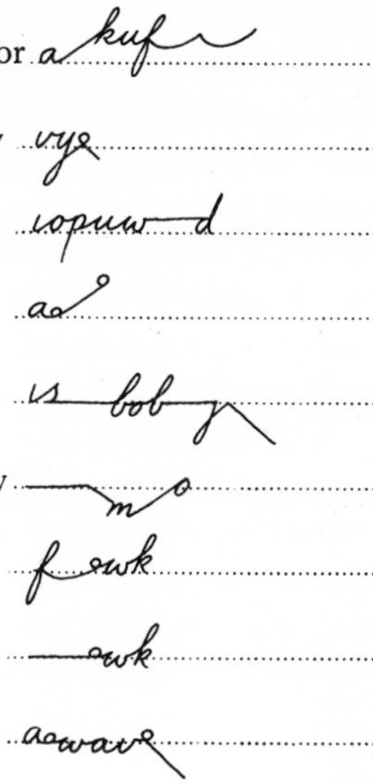

Dictation Passage 22(a) (see p. 124 for PitmanScript)

Gentlemen, Thank you for your note of yesterday. I regret[10] very much to learn that my new book *Organization and*[20] *Direction in the Factory* cannot be ready for publication on[30] the date originally suggested. I hope you will do all[40] you possibly can to have it published for the spring,[50] as it is at that time of the year that[60] large sales may be expected.

I wish, subject to your[70] approval, to have one hundred copies of the book as[80] soon as it is ready for free distribution to students[90] of the new College of Business Education in this town.[100] I think you know that my brother is the Principal[110] of this college, and I wish to make him a[120] present of the books. I shall be obliged if you[130] will kindly let me know the most favourable terms on[140] which you can allow me to purchase these books from[150] you. As has been arranged, I shall begin work this[160] week on the new edition of *Investigation into Division of*[170] *Labour*, and I hope to let you have the copy[180] for this during the first week in August. Very truly[190] yours, (191)

Dictation Passage 22(b) (see p. 125 for PitmanScript)

Dear Sir, As a result of a close examination of[10] the claim you made that the glass goods received from[20] us last week were delivered broken, we regret to inform[30] you that we do not find it possible to allow[40] your claim. You should, of course, have put in a[50] claim at once, as it is a rule with this[60] firm that the customer must check all glass goods at[70] the time of delivery and that he must not sign[80] the receipt for the goods before examining them. In this[90] case the young man who delivered the goods to you[100] tells us that he had to wait fifteen minutes before[110] you returned the receipt to him. We have also seen[120] the manager of our packing department, and he states that[130] the usual examination of the package took place before it[140] left his department.

With these facts before us, we cannot[150] allow your claim, but in view of the pleasant relations[160] between us in the past we shall be happy in[170] this case to allow you thirty per cent off the[180] invoice price of the goods. Kindly let us know by[190] return of post if you accept this offer, and at[200] the same time inform us whether you wish us to[210] deliver a set of glass to take the place of[220] the damaged goods. Yours truly, (225)

Facility Practice 22 (see p. 139 for Key)

(a)
(b)
(c)
(d)
(e)

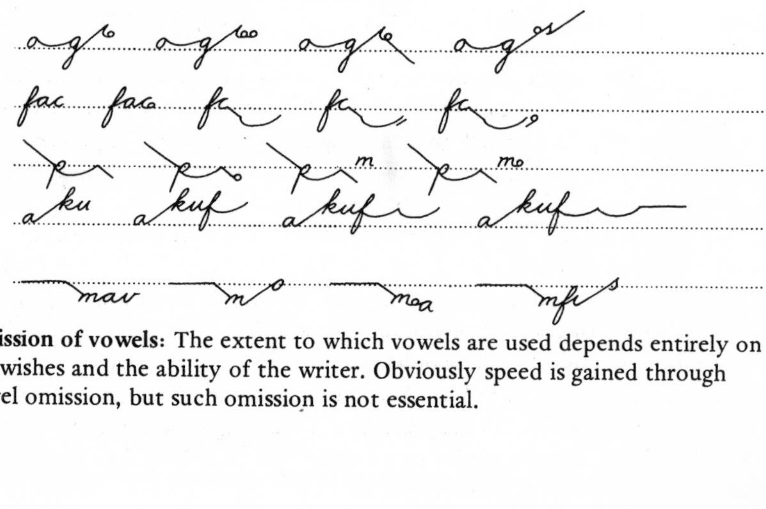

Omission of vowels: The extent to which vowels are used depends entirely on the wishes and the ability of the writer. Obviously speed is gained through vowel omission, but such omission is not essential.

Vocabulary drill

nothing	ng	on	o
November	v	once	wu, w
now	ou	one	1, wu, w
number	no	only	o
object	objc	open	op
observation	obe vs	operate	op a
October	oc	opinion	op
of	v	opportunity	op, op
off	of	or	o
offer	of	order	o
office	ofs	organize	o g
official	ofis	other	ul
often	of	ought	au
oh / owe	o	our	ou
oil	oi	out	ou
old	o	over	ov

Drill based on Dictation Passage 23

advance	a	catch	cac, cc
vacation	vcas, vcs	entirely	e

as soon as possible	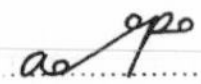	course of action	
I wished		this was	
I found			

Dictation Passage 23 (see p. 126 for PitmanScript)

When my examination was over my one thought was to get out of town as soon as possible. I had everything ready in advance, and on the first day of the vacation I left the house at six o'clock and set off on what I wished to be the best vacation I had ever had.

I thought that few people would be about at this early hour but, to my surprise, I found when I reached the station that several hundred people were already there, all of them no doubt with the same thought of the happy days of the vacation before them. No room was available in the train which I had set out to catch, and I was told that I must wait with a number of other people for this train to leave and the next one to come in. This led me to decide on an entirely different course of action. I thought that I would find a train with very few people in it, get into it, and let it take me to any place to which it might be going. This was the beginning of what turned out to be a most original vacation. (200)

Facility Practice 23 (see p. 139 for Key)

(a) 

(b) 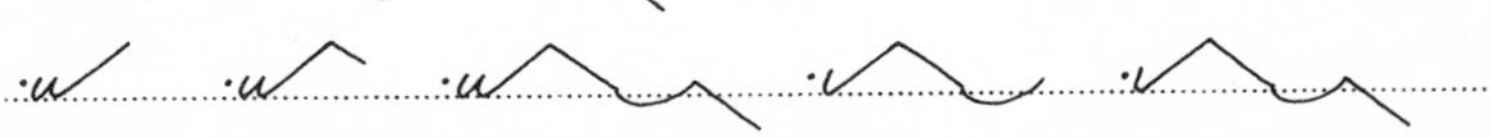

(c) 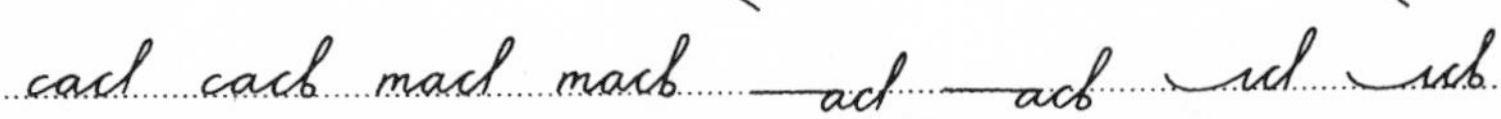

(d) 

(e) 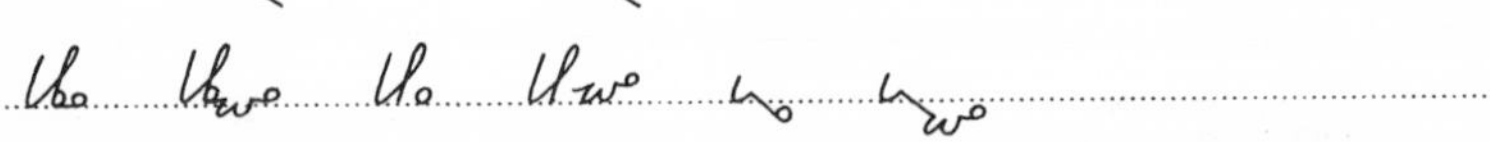

Spelling: The words *benefit*, *develop*, *potato* and *tomato* have no final *e*. The words *respite*, *envelope* and *toe*, on the other hand, do have a final *e*. It is worth while to memorize the spelling of all these words. In PitmanScript they are written:

(a) 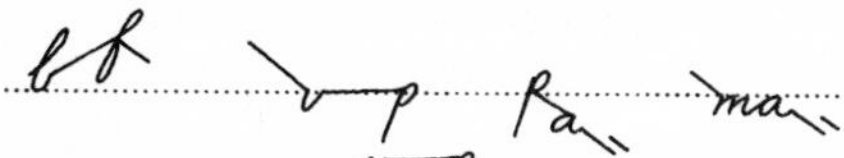

(b) 

Vocabulary drill

owing
own
page
paint
paper
part
particular
party
pass
pay
peace }
piece }
penny
people
perfect
perhaps
person
picture
place
plain }
plane }
plan
plant
play
please
pleasure
point
political
poor
position
possible
pound
power
present

Drill based on Dictation Passage 24

familiar
furniture
furnishing
glorious

opportunity
co-operate
representative
quantity
piano

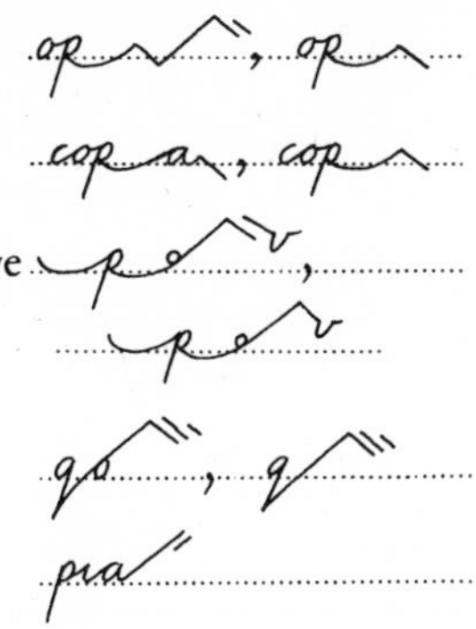

Company Limited
well worth
no longer
that you can
out of date
first-class
see us
you may exchange
please write

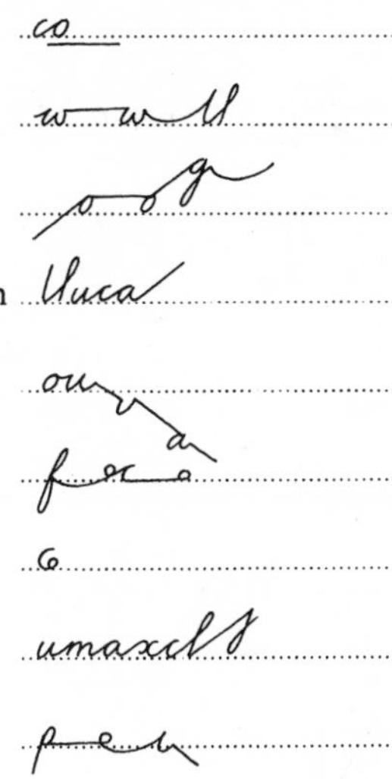

Dictation Passage 24 (see p. 126 for PitmanScript)

Are you familiar with the latest service offered by the[10] Modern Furniture Company Limited? If not, it will be well[20] worth your while to spend a little time in studying[30] the enclosed booklet *Exchange Service in Furnishing Homes.* No longer[40] is it necessary to keep old furniture in your home[50] when you long for something new, something both practical and[60] beautiful.

It is common knowledge that you can exchange your[70] old car for a modern one. We are now offering[80] you this glorious opportunity to exchange your old and out[90] of date furniture for delightful modern furniture of first-class[100] quality, and so secure a perfectly planned home.

Come along[110] and see us, and we will gladly co-operate with you[120] by an exchange of ideas and by making suggestions of[130] real value. If you prefer it, our representative will call[140] on you at your home at any time convenient to[150] you and make an inspection of the furniture you wish[160] to exchange. The price quoted by him will be taken[170] from the price of the new furniture you choose, and[180] the balance is payable on easy terms. You may exchange[190] any quantity of furniture, from a single article such as[200] a piano, to the furniture of the entire house.

Please[210] write or call. You are not obliged to purchase. (219)

Facility Practice 24 (see p. 140 for Key)

(a) 

(b) 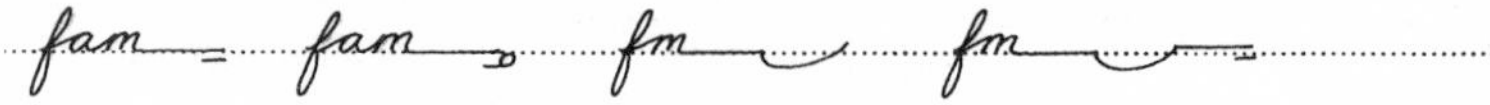

(c) 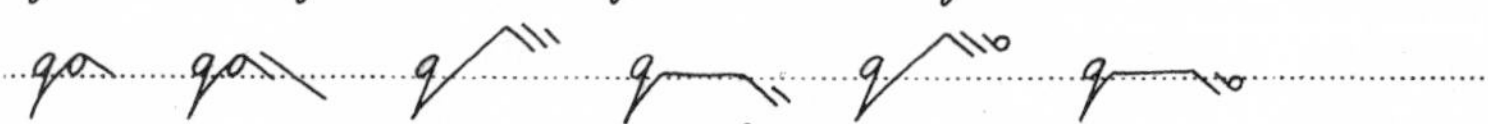

(d) 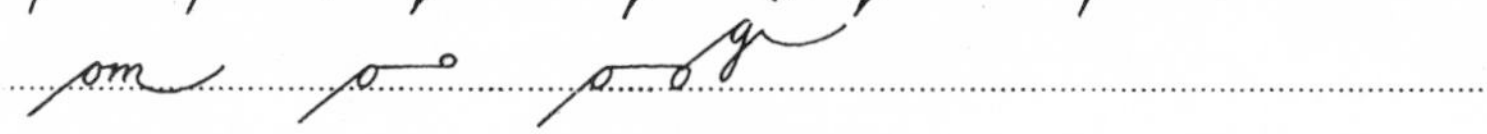

(e) 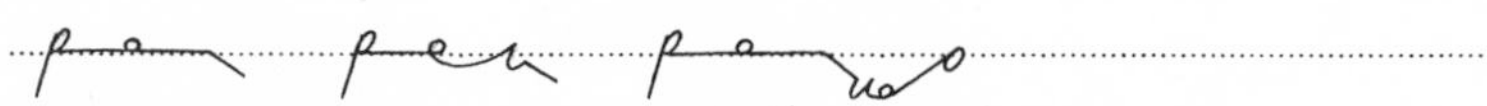

(f) 

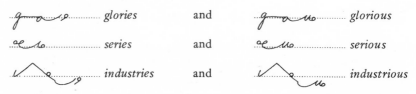

The termination *-ture* may generally be written , as in 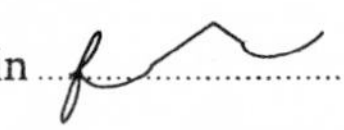 *furniture.*

 is sufficient to represent *-ious*. Compare:

	*glories*	and		*glorious*
	*series*	and	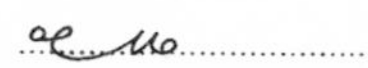	*serious*
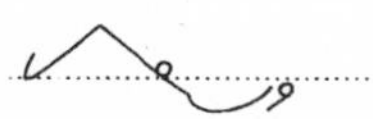	*industries*	and		*industrious*

If two *t* sounds are not linked by a stressed vowel, the strokes for them are disjoined, as in 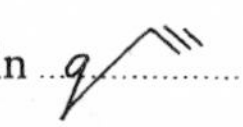 *quantity*. (Notice that the disjoined dash for a final vowel is not so long as downstroke T.) The disjoined dash is repeated for a double vowel, as in 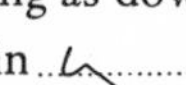 *idea.*

Vocabulary drill

price

principal / principle

probable

product

profit

property

provide

public

publish

pull

purpose

put

quality

quarter

question

quick

quite

radio

rail

rate

rather

reach

read

real

reason

receive

recent

record

red

regard

regret

regular

Drill based on Dictation Passage 25

neglected

tired

normal

shoes

arrangements

description

individual

should be

in order to

well known

you may require

and we are confident

Dictation Passage 25 (see p. 127 for PitmanScript)

Foot comfort is frequently so seriously neglected that many women[10] find themselves tired before lunch. Walking is so important a[20] part of our normal life that every attempt should be[30] made to see that it is an easy action, made[40] without effort. Our special *Good Fit* shoes offer a short[50] cut to foot comfort. The woman who uses them can[60] walk easily, in complete comfort.

In order to make these[70] shoes well known in your district we have made arrangements[80] for your local stores to sell them during the present[90] month at twenty-five per cent below the usual price.[100] Give your feet a holiday. First read through the enclosed[110] booklet *Tired Before Lunch*, which gives a full description of[120] our shoes, with prices; then visit your local stores and[130] ask for our *Good Fit* shoes. Look out for the[140] special trade mark, which is on all our goods.

If[150] the manager of the store has not in stock the[160] particular size you may require, he can arrange to get[170] it for you within twenty-four hours. There are *Good*[180] *Fit* shoes to meet every individual need, and we are[190] confident that we can satisfy your special requirements. (198)

Facility Practice 25 (see p. 140 for Key)

(a)

(b)

(c)

(d)

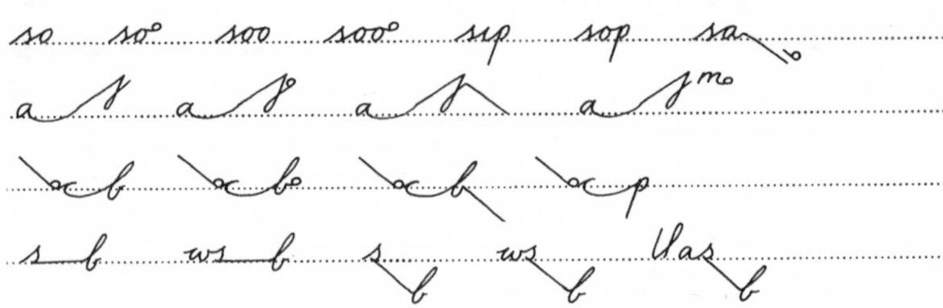

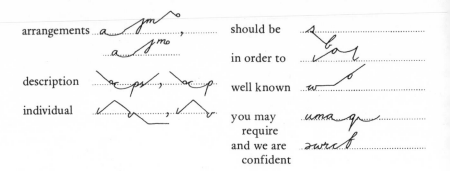

(e) 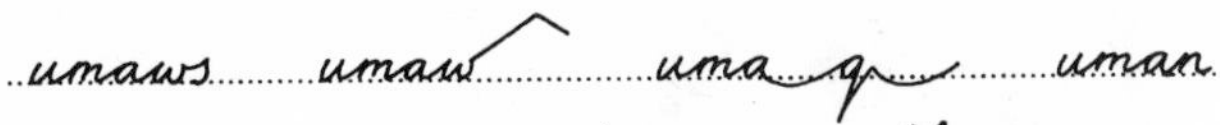

(f) 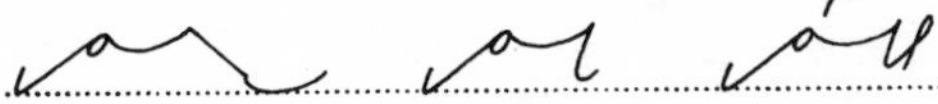

Spelling: Note that the following words all end in *-ible*: *visible*, *sensible*, *flexible*, *legible*, *edible*, *audible*. The PitmanScript forms are:

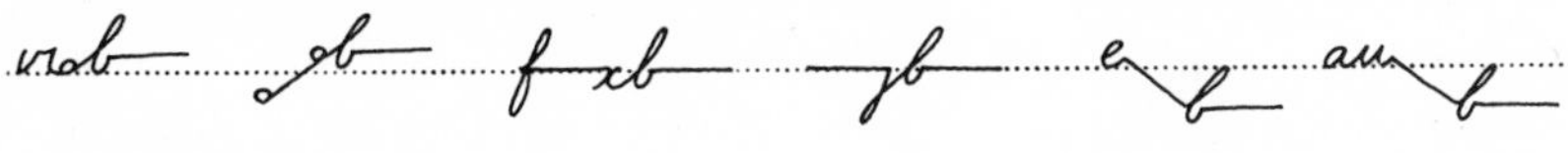

Unit 3

Passages of 200 words with unrestricted vocabulary

Vocabulary drill

relate

remark

remember

report

represent

require

respect

responsible

rest

result

return

right }
write }

river

road

rule

run

room

round

safe

said

sail }
sale }

same

satisfactory

Saturday

save

say

scene }
seen }

science

school		seem	
sea / see		self	

Drill based on Dictation Passage 26

season		take into consideration	
justified		for the year	
modest		under review	
reflects		to some extent	
review		once more	
unfortunately		we were able to	
inevitable		I must mention	
production		we feel confident	
acquired			
substantial			
established			
reputation			
installed			
investment			
concluding			
financial			

Dictation Passage 26 (see p. 128 for PitmanScript)

When we take into consideration the difficulties of the past[10] season we are justified in considering the results as satisfactory.[20] There is a modest increase in the trading profit for[30] the year, and this reflects great credit upon all of[40] our employees. During the first three months of the year[50] under review both our production and our sales exceeded all[60] previous records for a similar period. Unfortunately, this had the[70] inevitable result of causing prices to fall, and we found[80] it necessary to cut production to some extent. However, the[90] wide interests of your organization contributed to make the year[100] a good one, and we were able to resume full[110] production once more. In January last we acquired a substantial[120] interest in the undertaking at Glasgow. This is a very[130] old-established business with a high reputation for the quality[140] of its output. The factory is in a first-class[150] position, and recently very modern plant was installed. We feel[160] confident that this will prove a very satisfactory form of[170] investment. I must mention before concluding my remarks that the[180] trading results for the first three months of the current[190] financial year fully justify us in a feeling of confidence. (200)

Facility Practice 26 (see p. 140 for Key)

(a) 

(b) 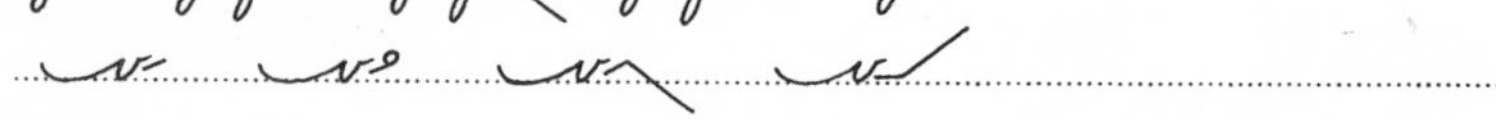

(c) 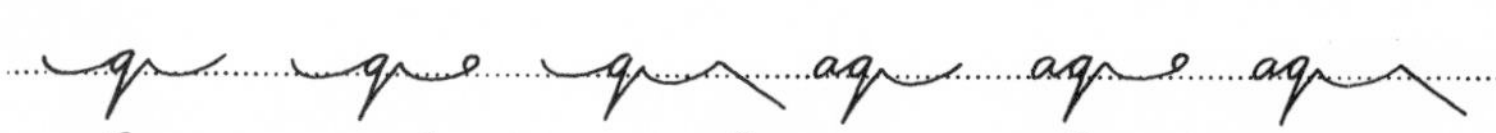

(d) 

(e) 

(f) 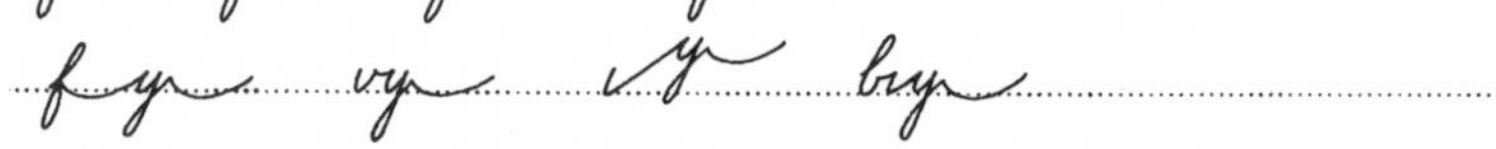

Some pairs of forms

inevitable 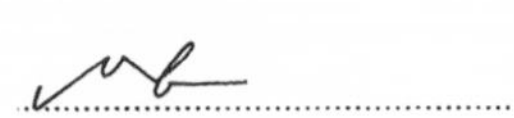 unavoidable 

employ  employee 

products		produce	
extent		extend	
extension	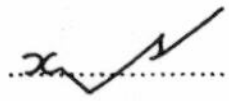	expansion	
contribute	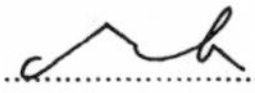	attribute	
plan	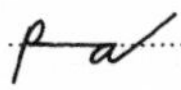	plant	

Vocabulary drill

sell	side
send	sign
sense	simple
sent	since
September	sir
serious	sit
serve	situation
service	six
set	size
several	small
shall	so / sow / sew
she	
ship	some / sum
short	soon
should	sort
show	sound

Drill based on Dictation Passage 27

further	upward
economy	interrupted

encouraging	
industrial	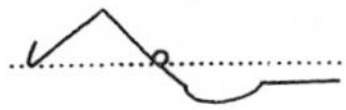
level	
average	
notwithstanding	
president	
index	
vitality	
recovery	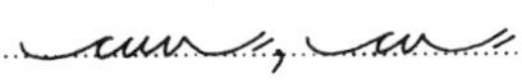
activity	
USA	
short time	
United States	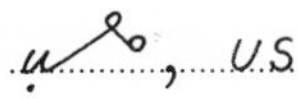
previous week	
which had been	
same time	

Dictation Passage 27 (see p. 129 for PitmanScript)

It is satisfactory to note that there was further evidence[10] last week that the economy of the USA[20] had resumed its upward movement, which had been interrupted for[30] a short time in January. The report of the United[40] States government for the previous week had suggested that there[50] would be an improvement. The report shows an encouraging gain[60] in the numbers in full employment between mid-January and mid-February.[70] Industrial production was again back at the high level it[80] had reached at the end of the year. The level[90] in December last was fifteen per cent above the average[100] of the last six years. At the same time personal[110] incomes had risen to a very high figure, notwithstanding the[120] very slight decline in January last. At a press conference[130] the President was asked about a complaint by labour leaders[140] that the business recovery seemed to be lacking in strength.[150] His reply was that the business index figures were not[160] as high as he had hoped they would be, but[170] that he had great confidence in the vitality of the[180] recovery.

It has been reported that the President's economic advisers[190] admit that business activity is still below annual average figures. (200)

Facility Practice 27 (see p. 140 for Key)

(a)
(b)
(c)
(d)
(e)

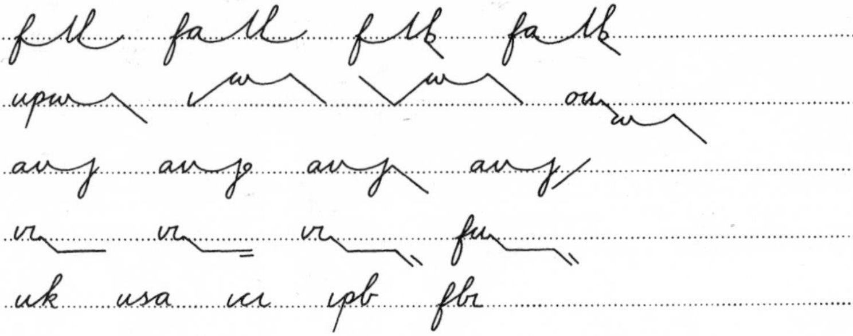

Note the use in (e) of small joined letters for names that are indicated by initial letters only. The writer can use capitals to indicate that the full name is required: U.S. *United States*.

Some pairs of forms

know		note	
further		farther	 *
father			
index		indicates	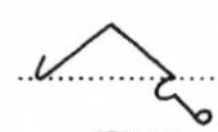
annually	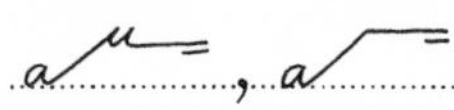	only	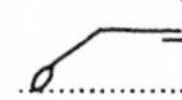

* The curve R is always included, whether or not the *r* is clearly sounded, as this helps rapid reading.

Vocabulary drill

south
speak
special
spend
stand
start
state
station
steal / steel
step
still
stone
stop
store
story
straight
strange

street
strong
subject
success
such
suggest
summer
Sunday
supply
support
sure
surprise
sweet
system
table
take

Drill based on Dictation Passage 28

recognized	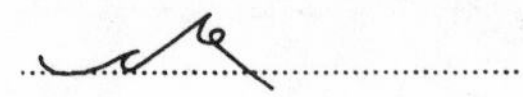	we want to	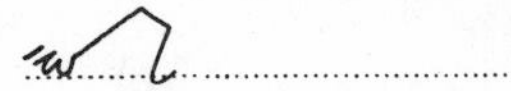
institution	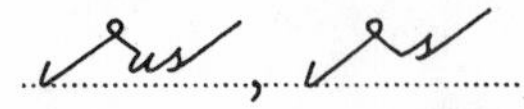	he must be	
courage		there is a	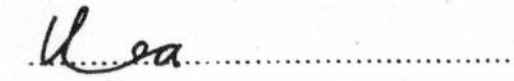
imagination	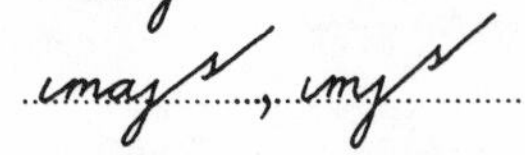	we would like	
capable	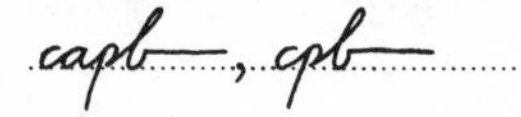	feel that	
problem	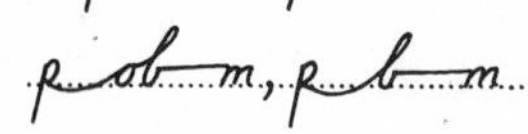	on our	
growing	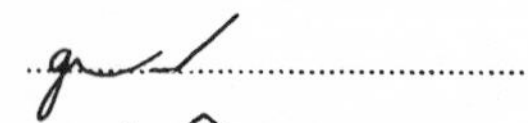	as well as	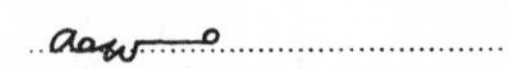
constantly	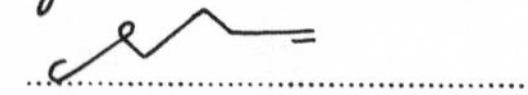	if you are	
promote			
superior			
qualifications	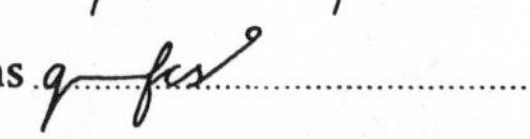		

Advanced writing: It will be noted that in many of the above forms, which represent words of two or more syllables, some vowels – or, in fast writing, all vowels – may be omitted. Thus, while in fast writing *problem* may be written , if you do include a vowel it will be the first one, since that is where the stress falls; thus: . In *promote*, written , the second vowel is included, since it is the one which is accented; this also helps to distinguish this form from that for *permit*, written 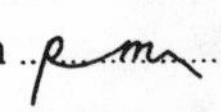.

In longer words such as *institution* and *superior*, most or all of the vowels can safely be omitted.

A fundamental rule of PitmanScript is that the writer need write only what is necessary for easy transcription. In the dictation passage which follows, there are many long words, and in parts of it the number of syllables is high in relation to the number of words. In cases such as this, abbreviation is helpful.

When abbreviating, it is better to discard vowels than consonants, as vowels are less important to legibility; but initial vowels must always be shown, as in

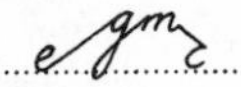 *enigmatic*, and a final vowel sound should be indicated, as in

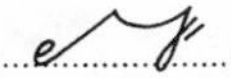 *energy*. Anyone doing a crossword and in possession of this much information would easily complete the word. It is the same process with transcription of long and abbreviated forms.

In the PitmanScript for Dictation Passages 28 to 32, an advanced style of writing is used, showing the omission of vowels or consonants and making full use of links.

Dictation Passage 28 (see p. 130 for PitmanScript)

We want to employ a man whose age is between[10] thirty and thirty-five years and who is a member[20] of a recognized engineering institution. The man we require must[30] have courage, skill, and imagination. He must be capable of[40] dealing with the broad issues of a problem while at[50] the same time not losing sight of the small details.[60] Our company is a large and growing concern, and it[70] is constantly expanding, so there is a place near the[80] top of this organization for the right man. We have[90] in our company at present many excellent men of average[100] ability, and we would like to promote one of these[110] men to the position here advertised. However, we do not[120] feel that there is on our staff at the present[130] moment just the person for whom we are looking. It[140] follows from this that the man whom we finally appoint[150] must be quite clearly superior to anyone on our existing[160] staff. He must have character as well as qualifications, and[170] must be energetic. We want a man that those in[180] all grades of the staff can look up to and[190] respect.

If you are such a man please contact us. (200)

Facility Practice 28 (see p. 141 for Key)

(a)
(b)
(c)

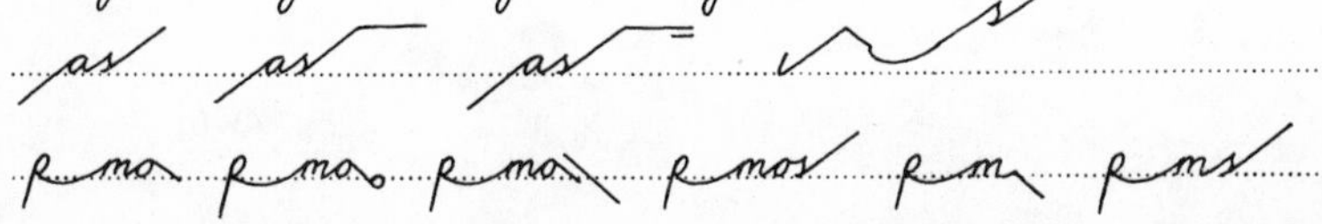

(d) 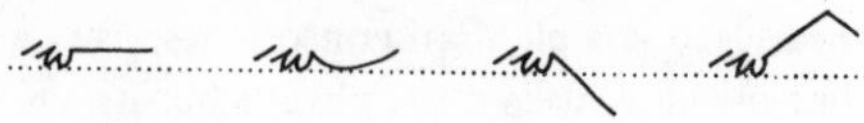

(e) 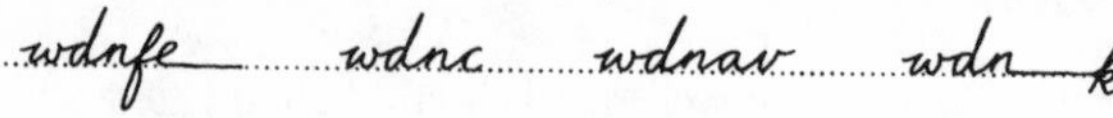

Some word endings

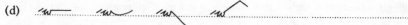

-ment	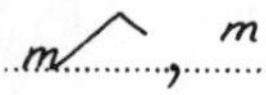	payment	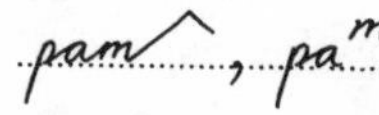
-mentally	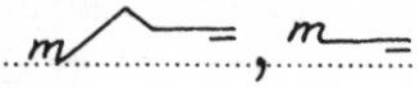	fundamentally	
-tal		total	
-tally		totally	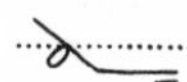
-tality		totality	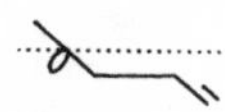
-ter		matter	
-ster		master	
-tend	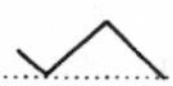	extend	
-ing		extending	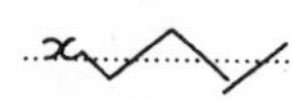
-ful		careful	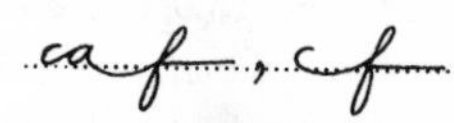
-fully		carefully	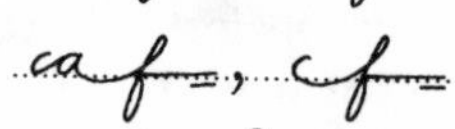
-fulness		carefulness	

These word endings can be written very quickly when the writer is familiar with them, and they should therefore be practised until such familiarity is gained.

Vocabulary drill

talk	think
tax	third
teach	this
tell	those
test	though
than	thought
thank	thousand
that	through
the	Thursday
their / there	till
therefore	time
them	to
then	together
these	told
they	tomorrow
thing	too

Drill based on Dictation Passage 29

hon.	insufficient
honourable	references

excessive	he should
hardship	has been given
originally	as high as
regional	400 per cent
occupy	has been done
normally	not only
Scotland	which is of
	in fact
England	less than
Wales	

Dictation Passage 29 (see p. 130 for PitmanScript)

The hon. Member made a number of points, but there[10] are still several more things which he should bear in[20] mind and to which insufficient weight has been given. First,[30] references have been made to increases as high as[40] 300 or 400 per cent. I have an example[50] of a house for which there has been an increase[60] of 300 per cent, but the rent is still[70] under 50 pence a week. No one would regard that[80] as being excessive. Also, everything has been done to avoid[90] hardship falling on the tenants. Not only has the very[100] small increase, which originally was to be for six months,[110] been extended for a whole year, but where the regional[120] housing board finds that somebody who has to occupy a[130] house is occupying one larger than he would normally need,[140] it is allowed to make a cut in excess of[150] 15 per cent. The next consideration, which is of great[160] importance, is that the average of the new rents in[170] Scotland will not be any greater; in fact, it will[180] probably be rather less than the average level of rents[190] for similar types of houses in England and in Wales. (200)

Facility Practice 29 (see p. 141 for Key)

(a) 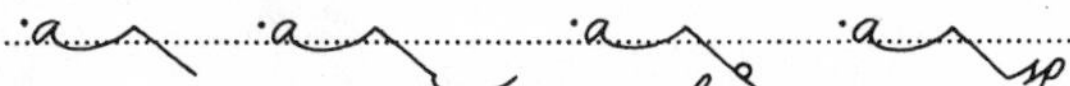

(b) 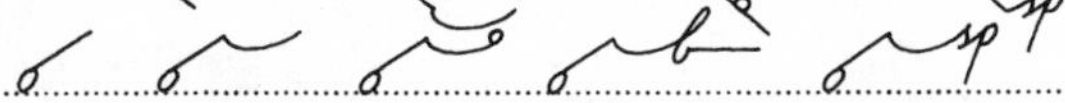

(c) 

(d) 

(e) 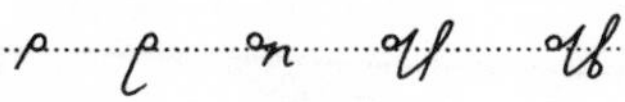

Some word endings

-shun		fashion	
-cial		social	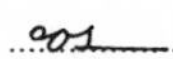
-sher		pressure	
-less		careless	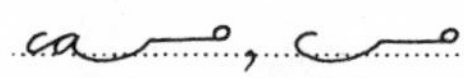
-lessly		carelessly	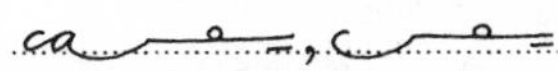
-lessness		carelessness	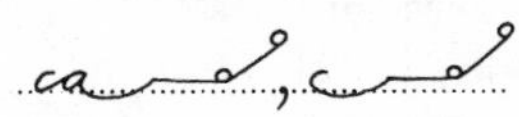
-rity		majority	
-lity		ability	
-gical	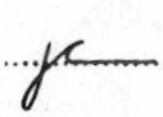	logical	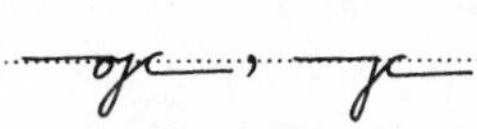

These word endings should also be practised until they can be written quite naturally – as naturally as ordinary longhand.

Vocabulary drill

touch		use	
towards		usual	
town		value	
trade		very	
train		view	
trouble		voice	
true		walk	
trust		want	
truth		war	
try		warm	
Tuesday		was	
turn		waste / waist	
under		watch	
until		water	
up		way / weigh	
us		we	

Drill based on Dictation Passage 30

civil		strike	
servants		Europe	

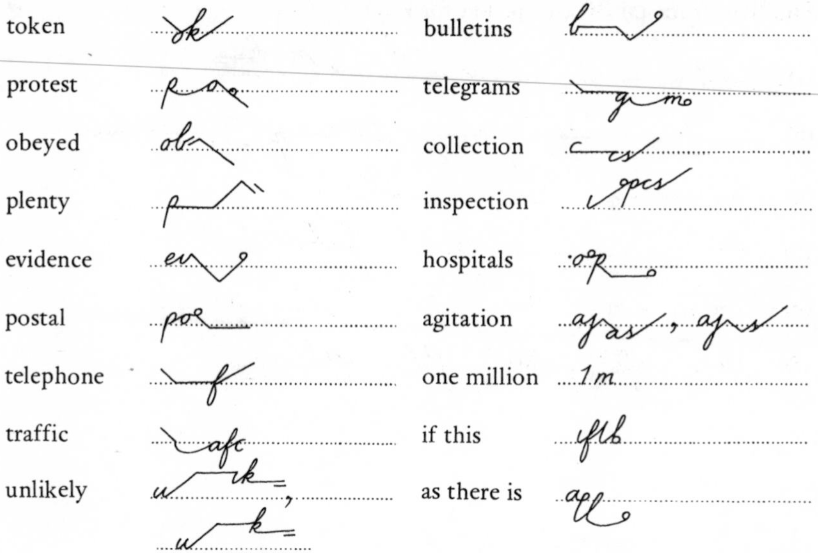

token
bulletins
protest
telegrams
obeyed
collection
plenty
inspection
evidence
hospitals
postal
agitation
telephone
one million
traffic
if this
unlikely
as there is

Dictation Passage 30 (see p. 131 for PitmanScript)

More than one million civil servants have been called out[10] on a one-day strike in Europe as a token[20] protest against the authority's refusal to give them a wage[30] increase of about five per cent. If this call is[40] generally obeyed, as there is plenty of evidence that it[50] will be, it means that the hard hit services will[60] be the postal and telephone services, air traffic, and all[70] general services. It is expected that there will be no[80] air traffic control at airports all day. It is unlikely[90] that there will be any European flights leaving or arriving[100] in England, and there will be no weather forecasts or[110] weather bulletins. Mail is not likely to be collected or[120] delivered. Telegrams and telephone calls will not be allowed unless[130] personal hardship can be proved. There will be no street[140] cleaning, no collection of tax, and no customs inspection. Teachers[150] employed by the Union will not be joining the strike,[160] and hospitals will continue the good work of taking care[170] of the sick.

Tomorrow's strike could be dangerous, if it[180] is really effective, and could lead to serious agitation among[190] the people at large. The position is certainly worth watching. (200)

Facility Practice 30 (see p. 141 for Key)

(a) 

(b) 

(c) 

(d) 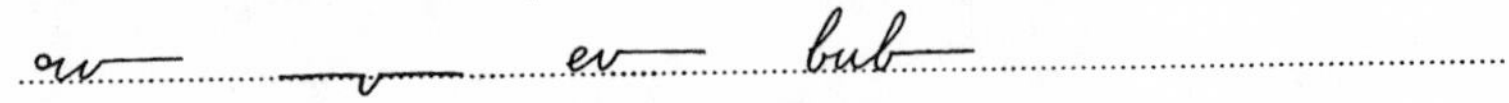

(e) 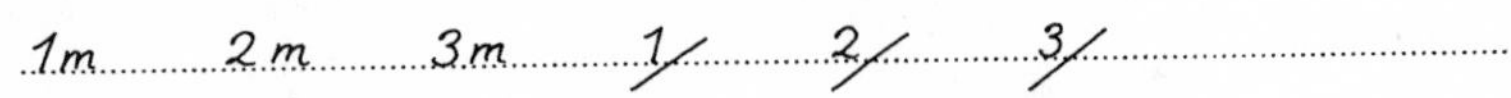

(f) 

Vocabulary drill

weak, week	
weather	
Wednesday	
well	
went	
were	
west	
what	
when	
where	
whether	
which	
while	
white	
who	
whole	
whom	
whose	
why	
wide	
will	
window	

Drill based on Dictation Passage 31

agencies	
recruited	
universities	
comprehensive	
technical	
selection	
clever	
executive	
first of all	
more than	
who will be able to	
can we say	

we shall have	ws av	fifteen thousand	15 ll
one thousand	1 ll	for us	f s

Dictation Passage 31 (see p. 132 for PitmanScript)

I want first of all to give you a few[10] figures. These figures were obtained by sending out forms to[20] be filled in by various agencies. No doubt some of[30] you who are here tonight will remember this particular form. Some[40] of the results are surprising. According to figures based on[50] the answers received we now employ nearly fifteen thousand people.[60]

I have here a chart which shows that we recruited[70] during the year more than one thousand young people direct[80] from schools or universities. Some came from art schools, some[90] from public schools. Others, of course, were recruited from comprehensive[100] schools and technical colleges.

An important question for us to[110] ask is whether our present methods of staff selection provide[120] us with the people who will be able to climb[130] to the top and to form the executive class of[140] the future. We certainly need a large number of clever[150] and able people at the top, and for the most[160] part we can secure them only by ensuring that we[170] take in the right people in the beginning. Can we[180] say that our selection of staff ensures that we shall[190] have a sufficient supply of top people later on? (199)

Facility Practice 31 (see p. 141 for Key)

(a)

(b)

(c)

(d)

(e)

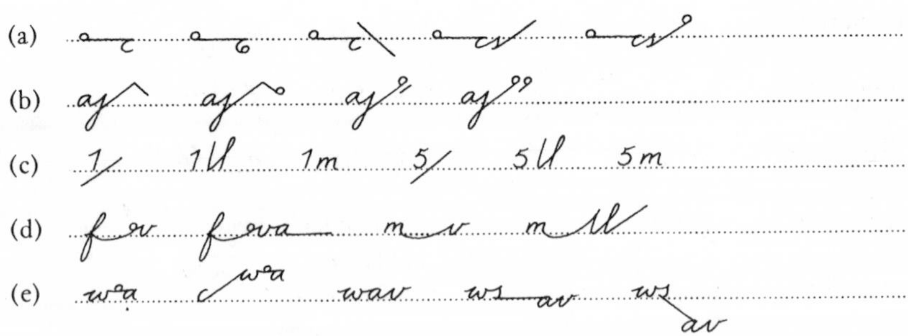

Some initial syllables

tele-		telephone	
con-		condition	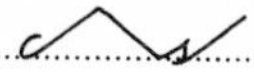
com-		commence	
accom-		accommodation	
intr-	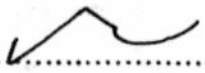	introduce	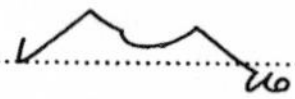
trans-		transfer	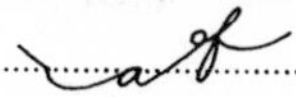
self-		self-made	

The following examples show the representation of negative prefixes. Compare:

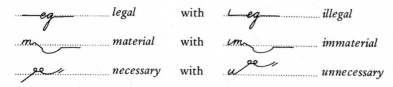

	*legal*	with		*illegal*
	*material*	with		*immaterial*
	*necessary*	with		*unnecessary*

(The inclusion of an initial vowel is a fundamental rule of PitmanScript.)

Vocabulary drill

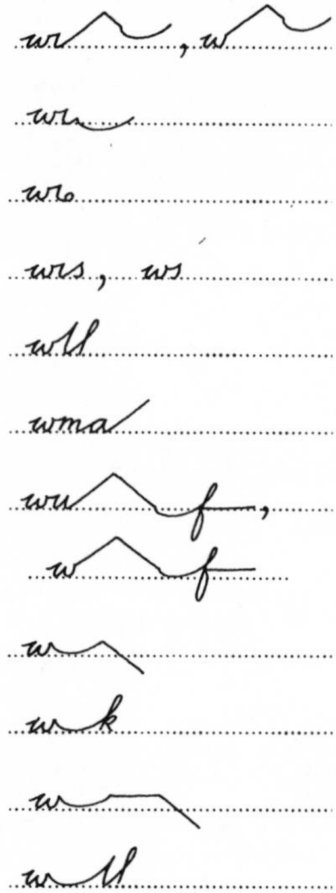

winter
wire
wise
wish
with
woman
wonderful
word
work
world
worth
would
write
wrong
yard
year
yes
yesterday
yet
you
young
your

Drill based on Dictation Passage 32

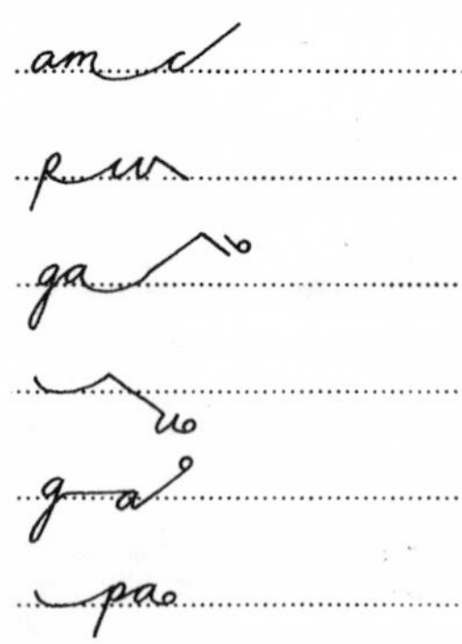

American
private
guarantees
reduce
glance
repays
New York
to this
it cannot be
there is no
it should not be
can be given

Dictation Passage 32 (see p. 133 for PitmanScript)

I have been encouraged to make this short review of[10] the present position because it has come to my notice[20] that reports are going round in New York that the[30] American authorities are working on a rather different solution to[40] this same problem.

We in this country are not alone[50] in being faced with a situation in which private investors[60] are not very eager to take up loans to provide[70] money for the more under-developed countries. In my opinion[80] the scheme which I have already outlined to you is[90] a very good one. While it cannot be applied to[100] every situation, there is no reason why it should not[110] be adapted to fit various cases in the future.

What[120] I have in view is a scheme by means of[130] which the same guarantees can be given to a private[140] investor in this field as are given to other investors.[150] It might be possible if this method were followed to[160] promote more loans through private people and private companies, and[170] thus reduce the burden on the state. A glance at[180] the list of countries which have received loans over the[190] last two years reveals a very interesting picture and well[200] repays study. (202)

Facility Practice 32 (see p. 142 for Key)

(a) (b) (c) (d)

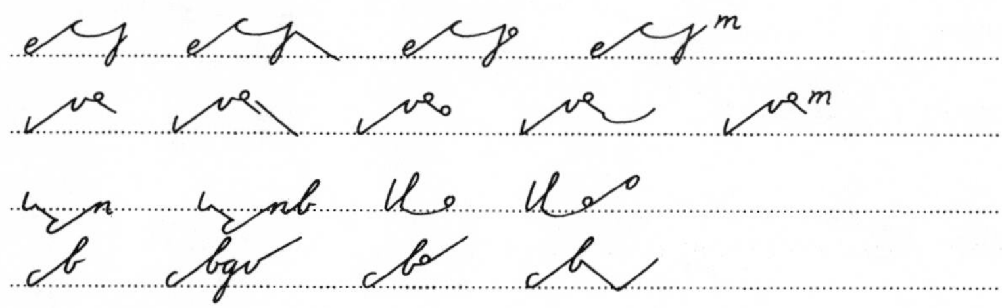

Some pairs of forms

accede  exceed 

adapt 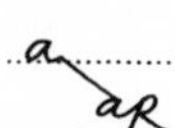 adopt 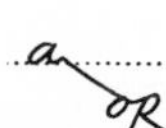

affect  effect 

allude  elude 

defer	differ
deprecate	depreciate
emit	omit
emigrate	immigrate
ingenious	ingenuous
perspective	prospective
prescribe	proscribe
succeed	secede
suite	suit
vacation	vocation

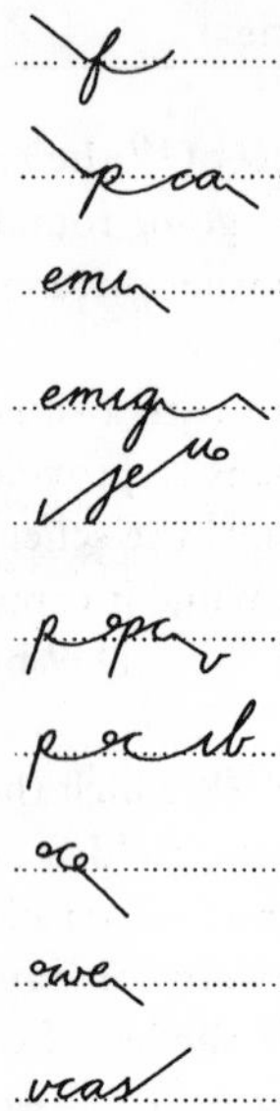

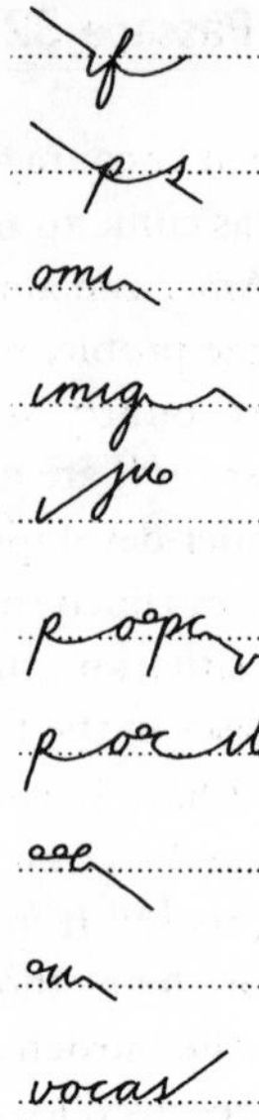

It is important for writers not only to be able to spell accurately but also to understand words which are not in common use. Writers can test themselves by trying to form sentences which contain all these words accurately used.

Tables of Joinings

These joinings should be practised until complete facility in writing them is achieved. This will considerably enhance the ability to write at speed.

Vowels with consonants

N: : *an*, *na*, *en*, *ne*, in, *ni*,

on, no, *un*, *nu*

L: : *al*, *la*, *el*, *le*, *il*, *li*,

ol, *lo*, *ul*, *lu*

S/Z: : as, *sa*, *es*, *se*, *is*, *si*,

os, so, us, *su*

T: : at, *ta*, *et*, *te*, it, *ti*,

ot, *to*, *ut*, *tu*

R: : *ar*, *ra*, *er*, *re*, *ir*, *ri*,

or, *ro*, *ur*, *ru*

D: : *ad*, *da*, *ed*, *de*, *id*, *di*,

od, *do*, *ud*, *du*

Consonants with consonants

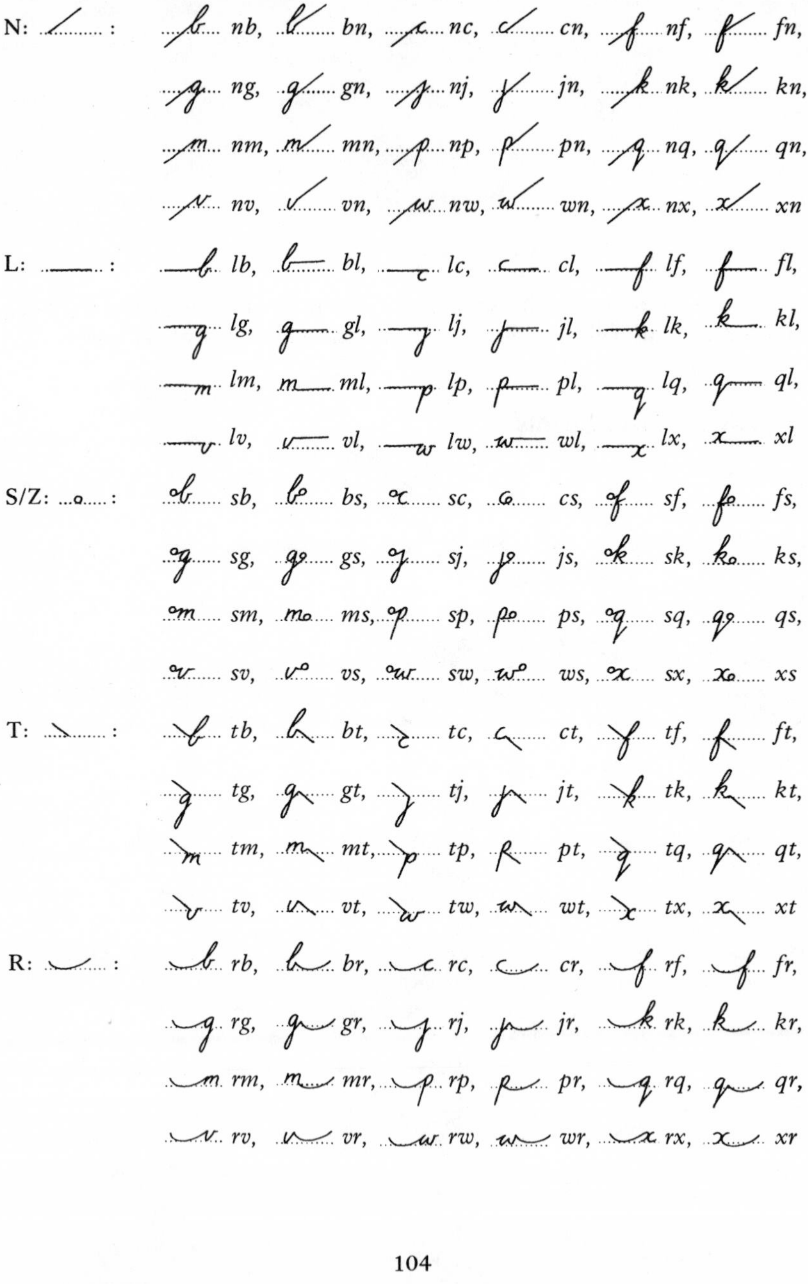
N: :
nb, bn, nc, cn, nf, fn,
ng, gn, nj, jn, nk, kn,
nm, mn, np, pn, nq, qn,
nv, vn, nw, wn, nx, xn
L: :
lb, bl, lc, cl, lf, fl,
lg, gl, lj, jl, lk, kl,
lm, ml, lp, pl, lq, ql,
lv, vl, lw, wl, lx, xl
S/Z: :
sb, bs, sc, cs, sf, fs,
sg, gs, sj, js, sk, ks,
sm, ms, sp, ps, sq, qs,
sv, vs, sw, ws, sx, xs
T: :
tb, bt, tc, ct, tf, ft,
tg, gt, tj, jt, tk, kt,
tm, mt, tp, pt, tq, qt,
tv, vt, tw, wt, tx, xt
R: :
rb, br, rc, cr, rf, fr,
rg, gr, rj, jr, rk, kr,
rm, mr, rp, pr, rq, qr,
rv, vr, rw, wr, rx, xr

D: :

db, *bd*, *dc*, *cd*, *df*, *fd*,

dg, *gd*, *dj*, *jd*, *dk*, *kd*,

dm, *md*, *dp*, *pd*, *dq*, *qd*,

dv, *vd*, *dw*, *wd*, *dx*, *xd*

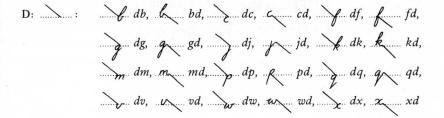

Notes on joinings

The letter *c* in PitmanScript is well curved, and is therefore quite distinct from *i*; thus:

= *cl*, = *il*, = *cs*, = *is*, = *cn*, = in

The combination *cr* is written in one sweeping curve:

= *cr*, = crash

The combination *ir* is written so as to show the join between the *i* and the curve R clearly; thus:

= *ir*, = wire

When circle S/Z is added after the vowels *a*, *e*, *i* and *u*, it should be placed low, as it is a waste of time to write a long lead-in stroke; thus:

= as, = *es*, = *is*, = us

PitmanScript Keys to Dictation Passages

Dictation Passage 1

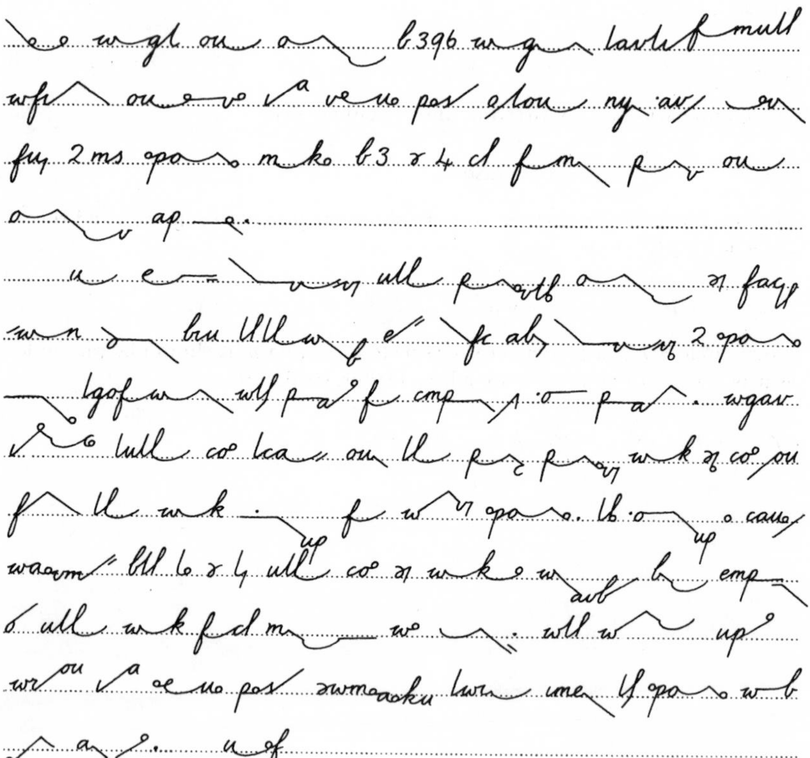

Dictation Passage 2

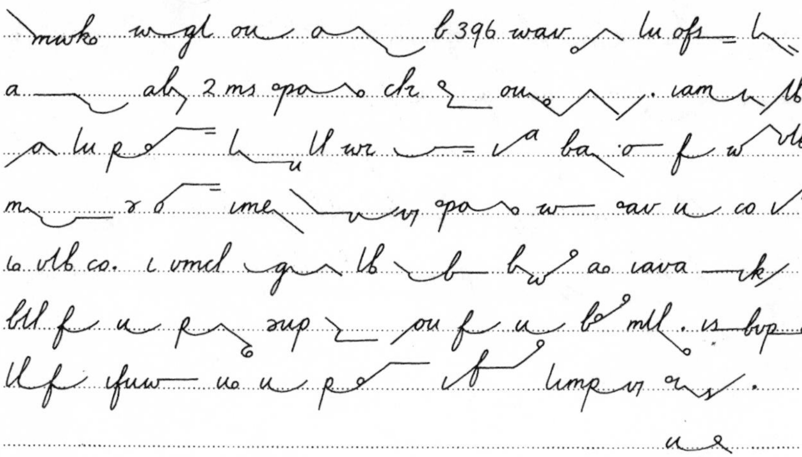

Dictation Passage 3

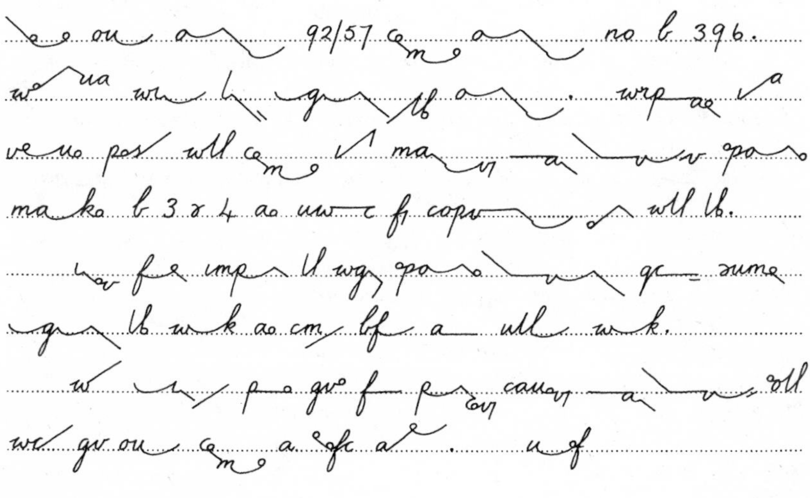

Dictation Passage 4

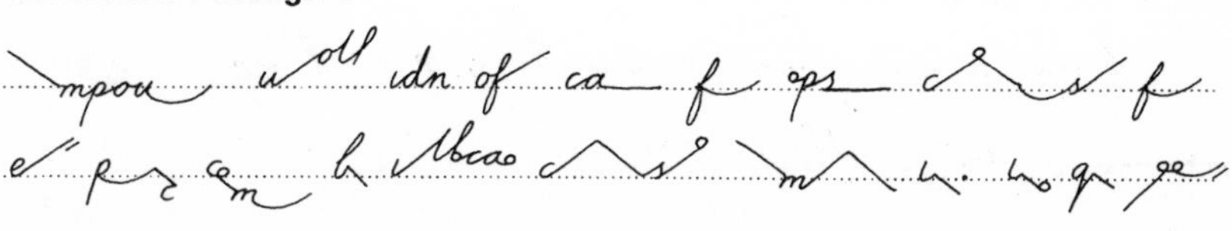

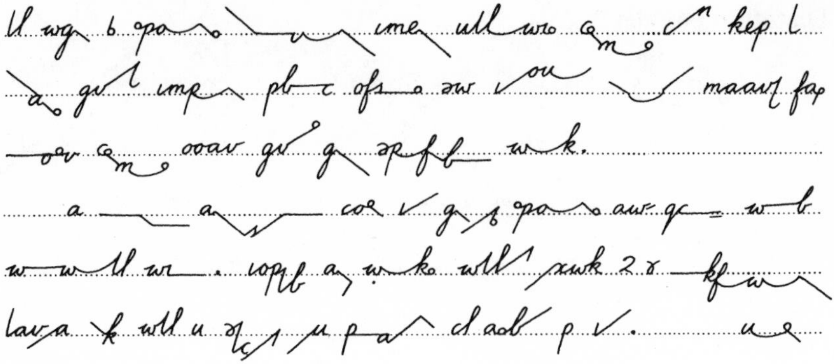

Dictation Passage 5

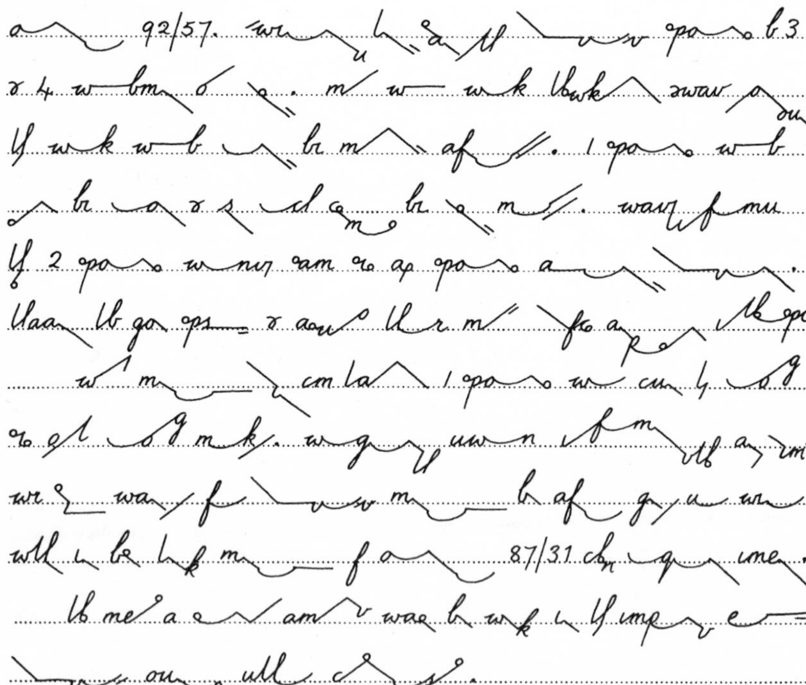

Dictation Passage 6

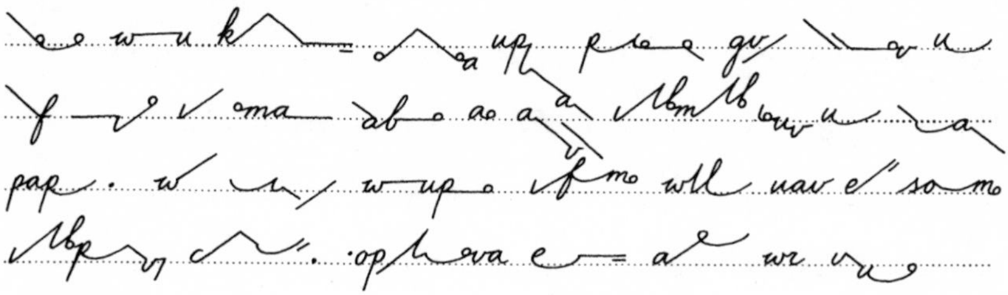

Dictation Passage 7

Dictation Passage 8

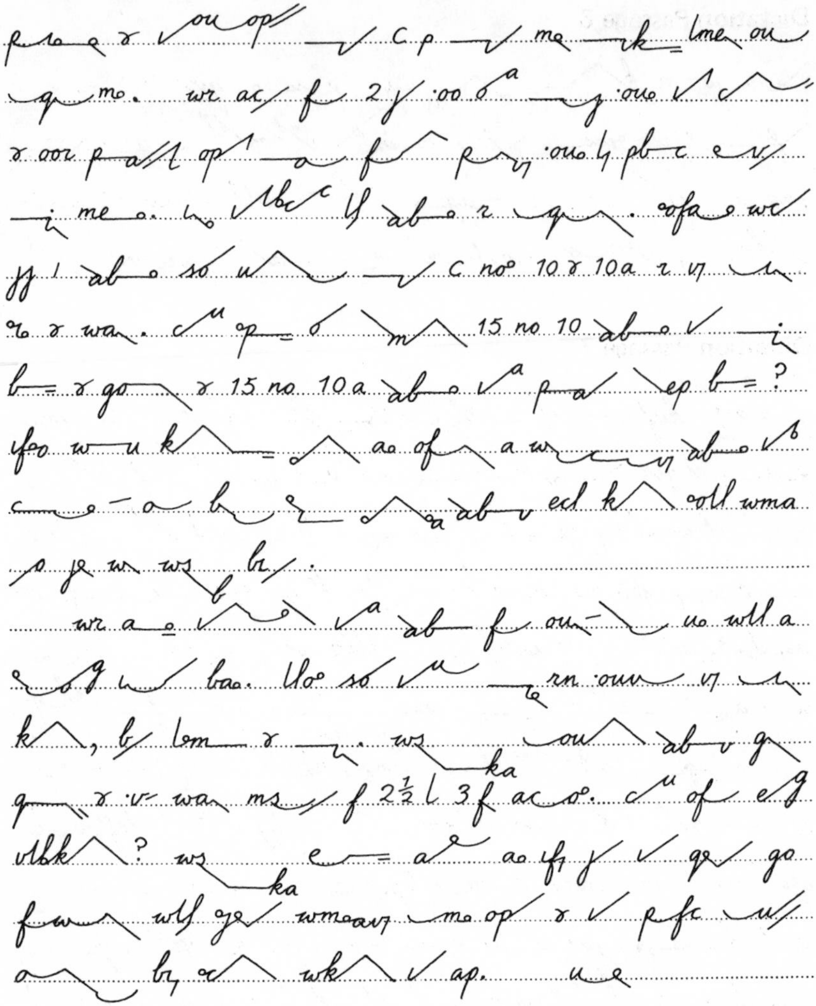

Dictation Passage 9

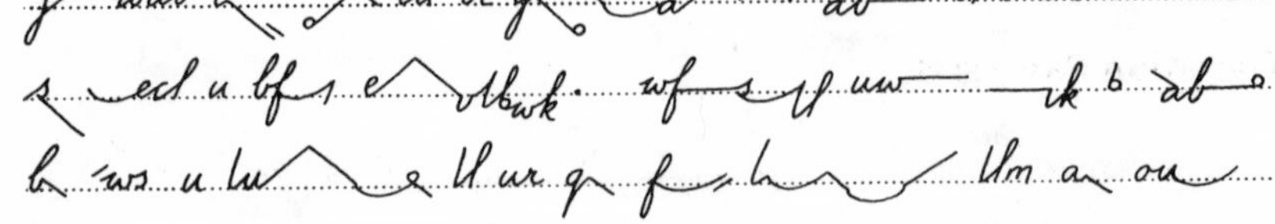

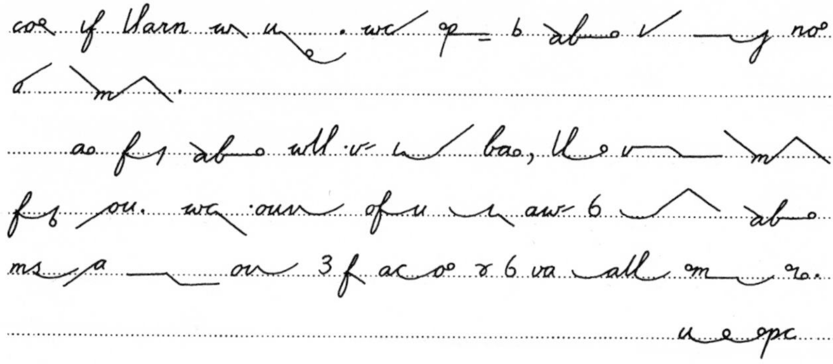

Dictation Passage 10

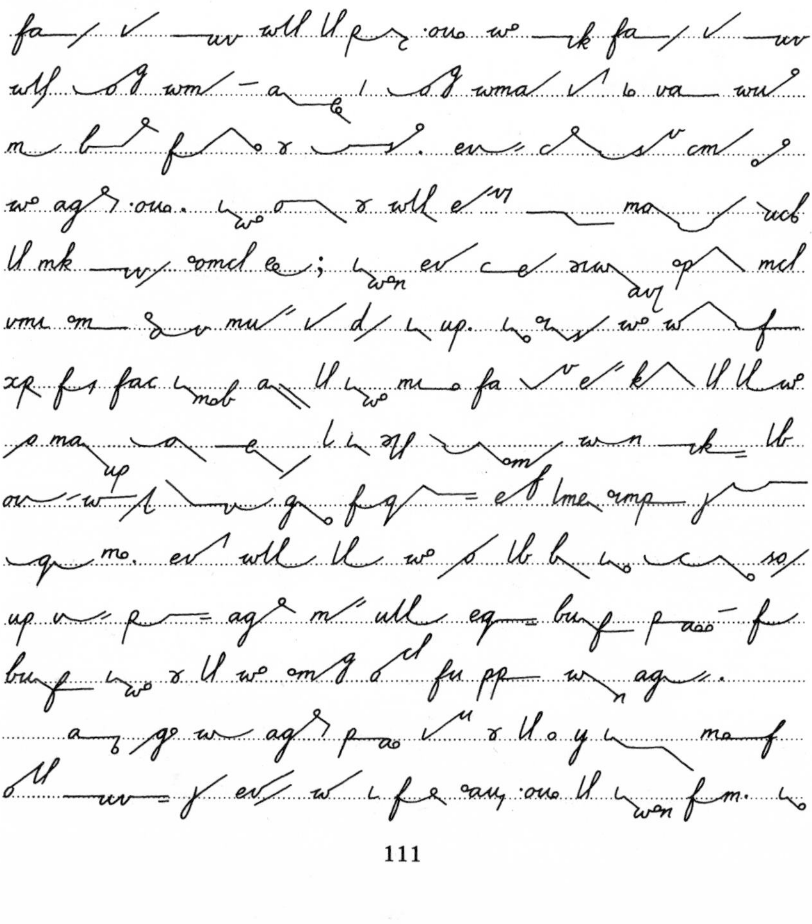

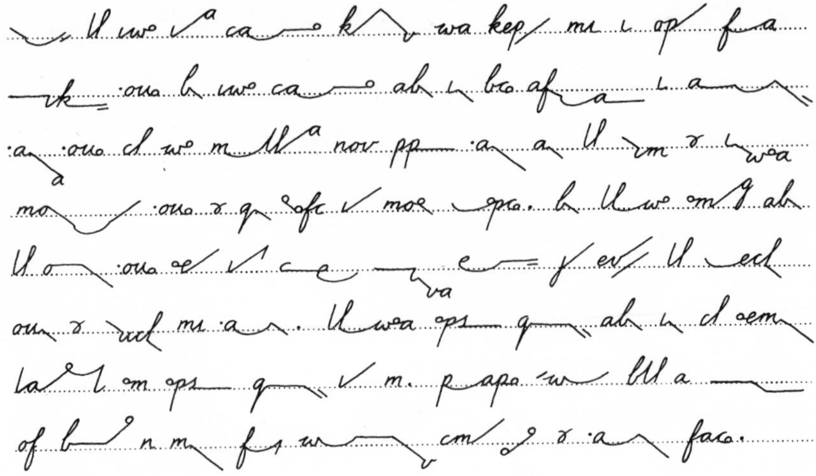

Dictation Passage 11

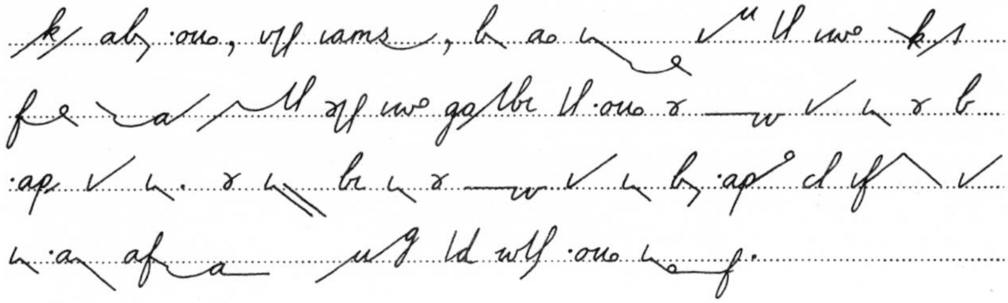

Dictation Passage 12

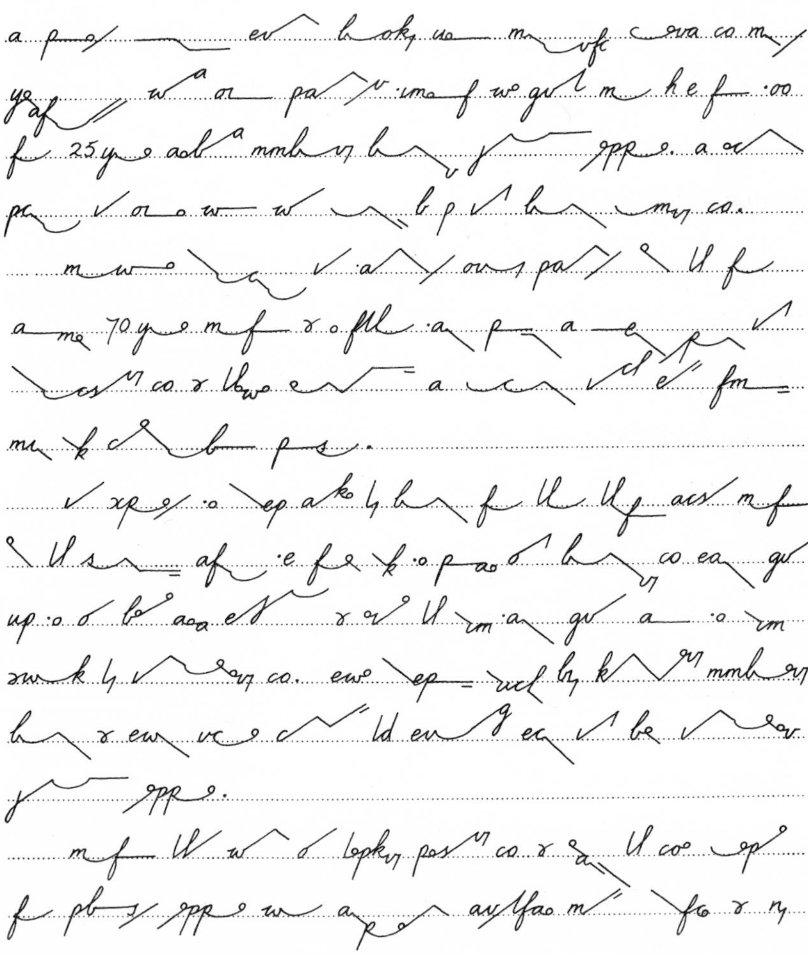

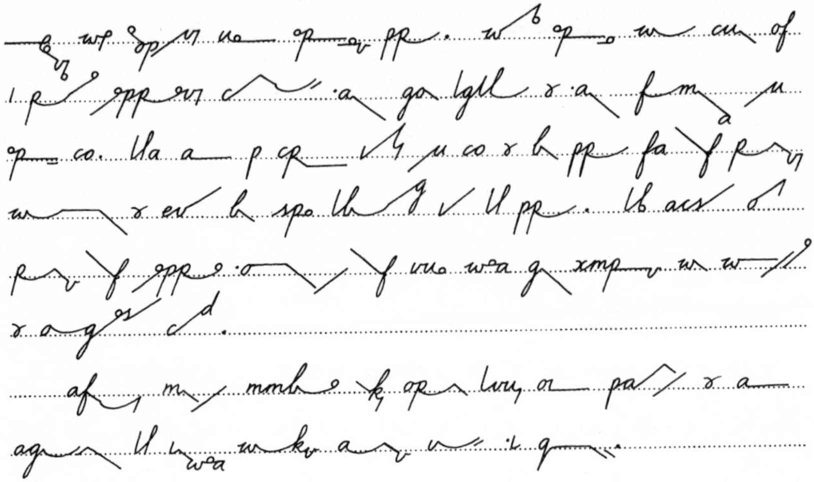

Dictation Passage 13

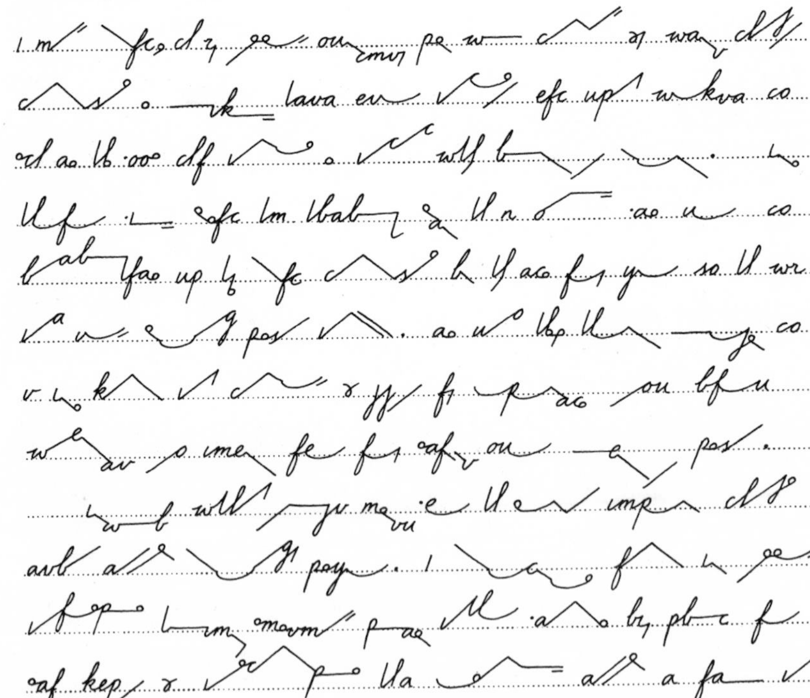

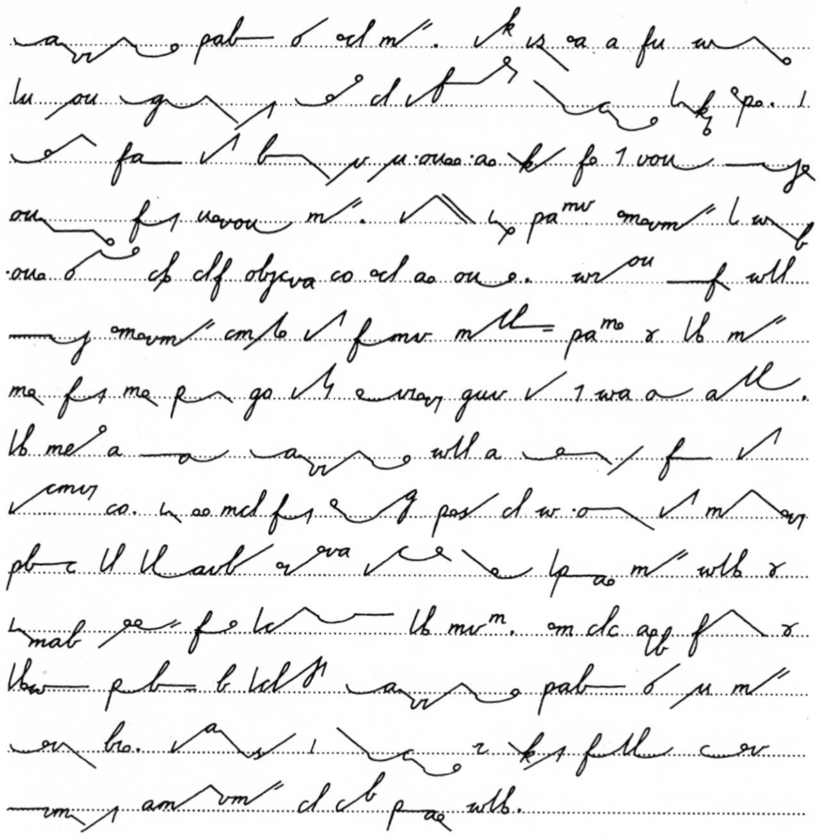

Dictation Passage 14

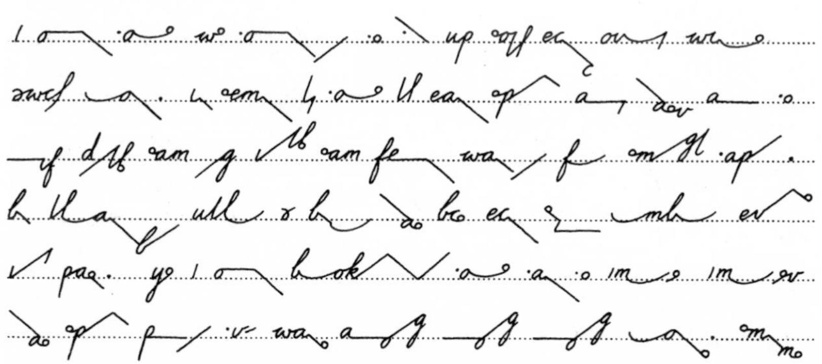

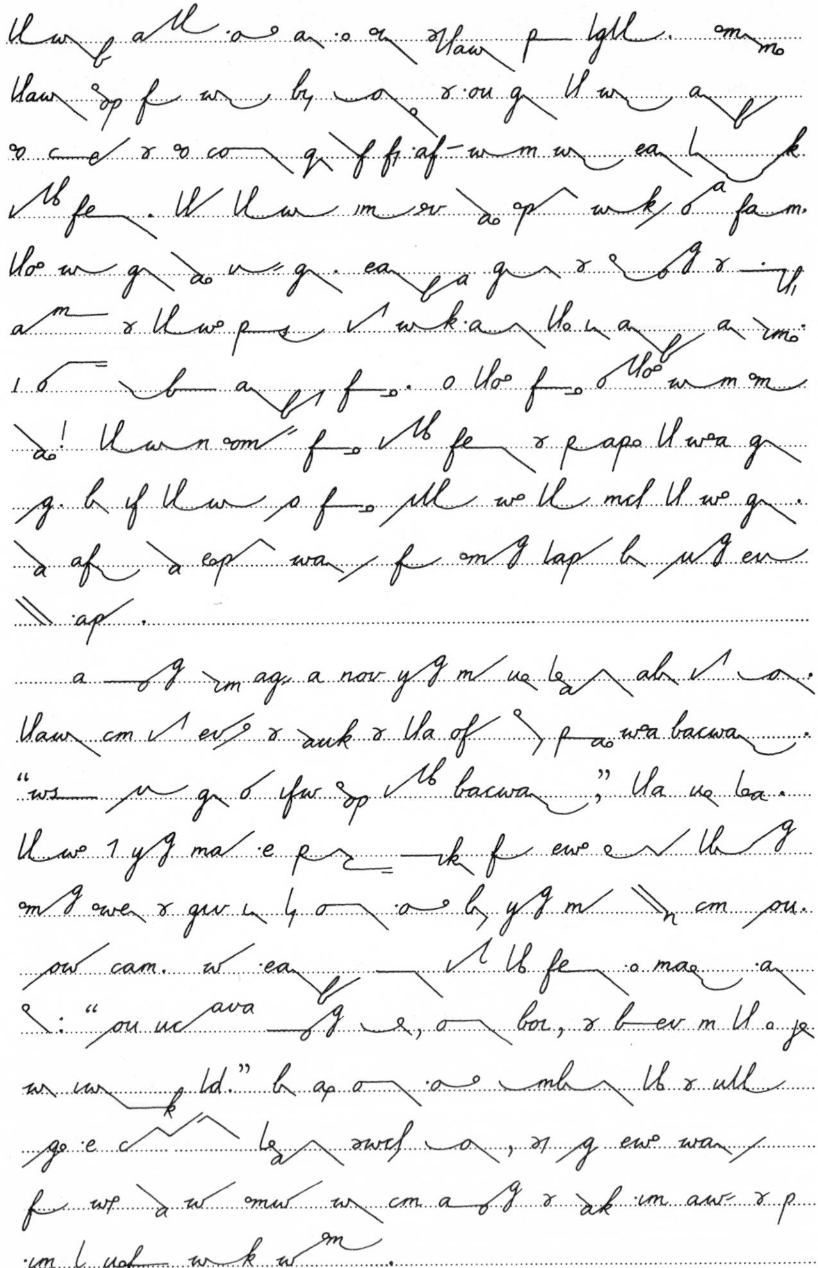

Dictation Passage 15

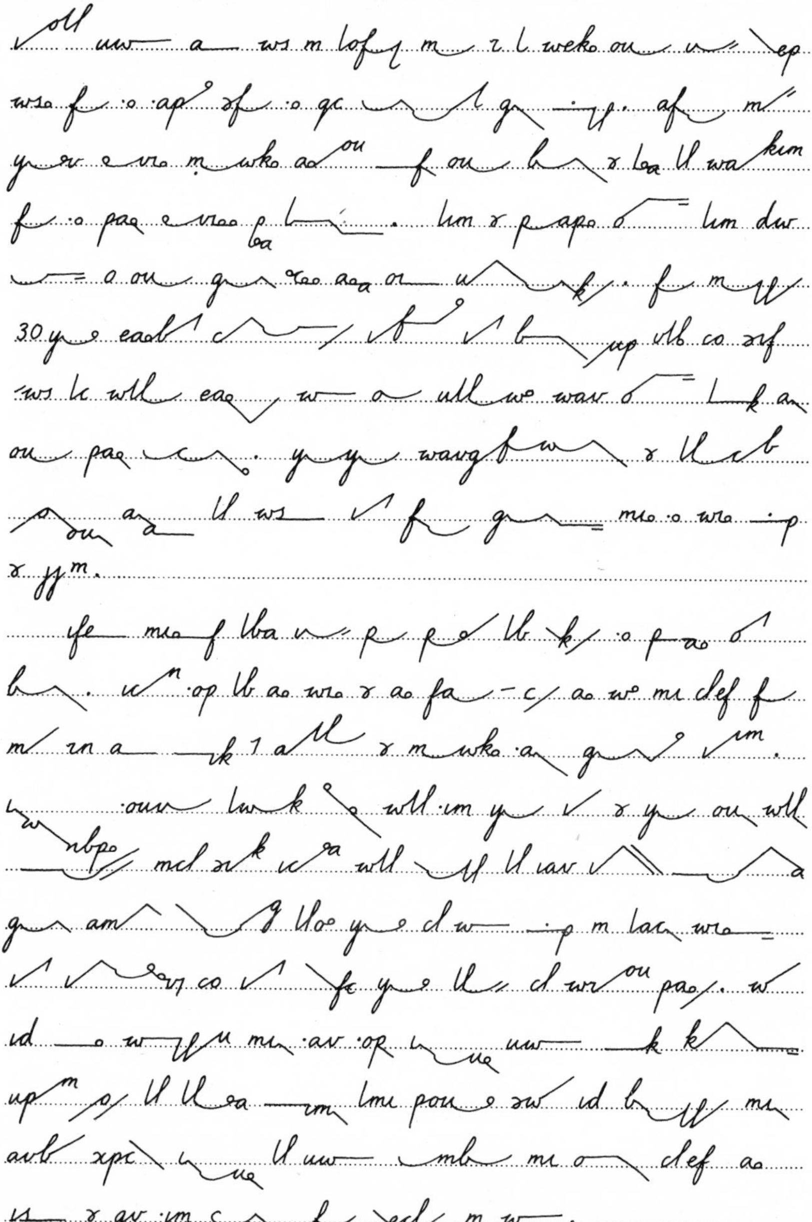

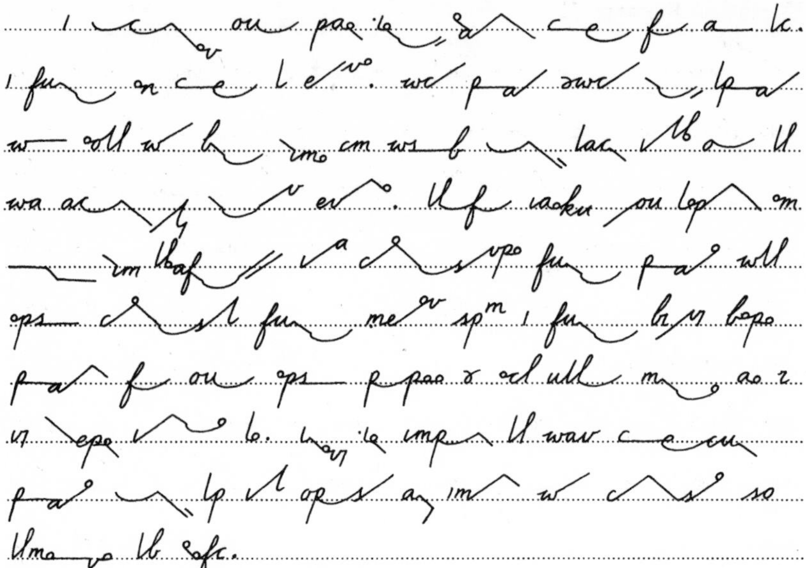

Dictation Passage 16(a)

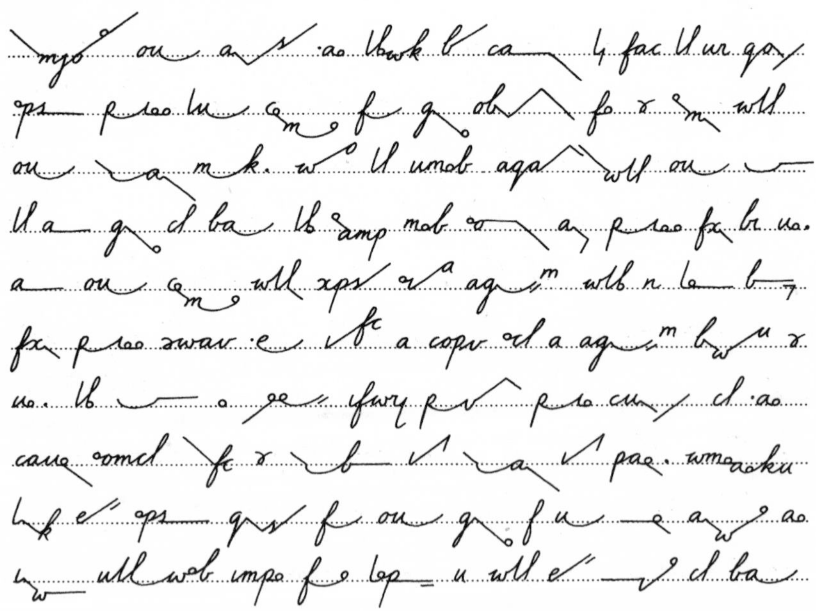

Dictation Passage 16(b)

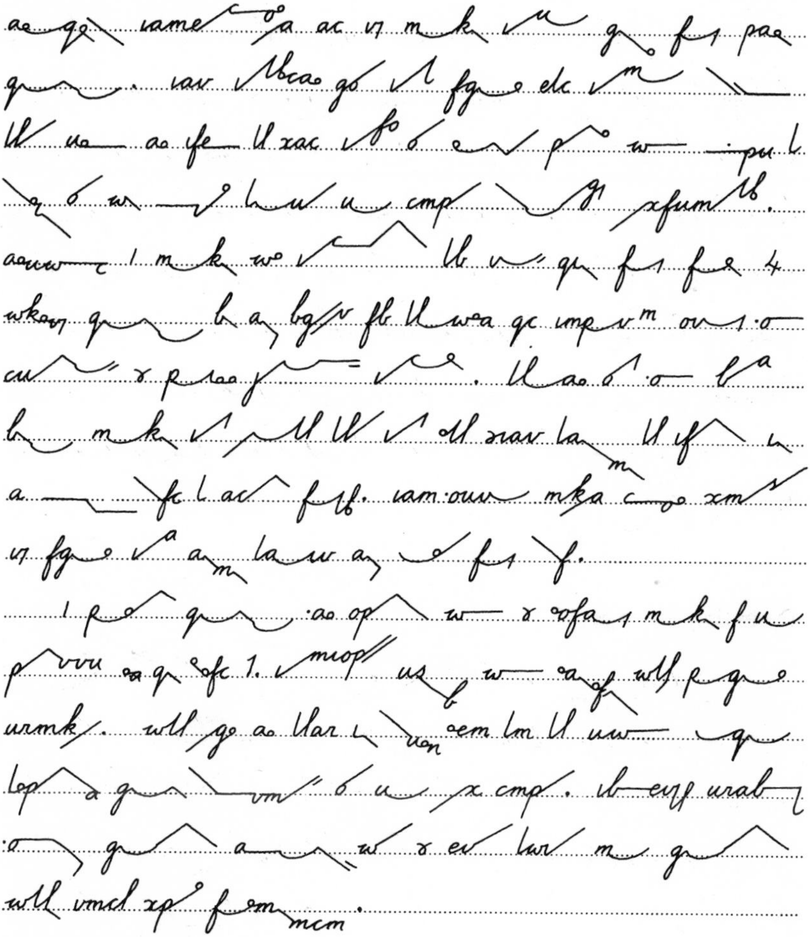

Dictation Passage 17

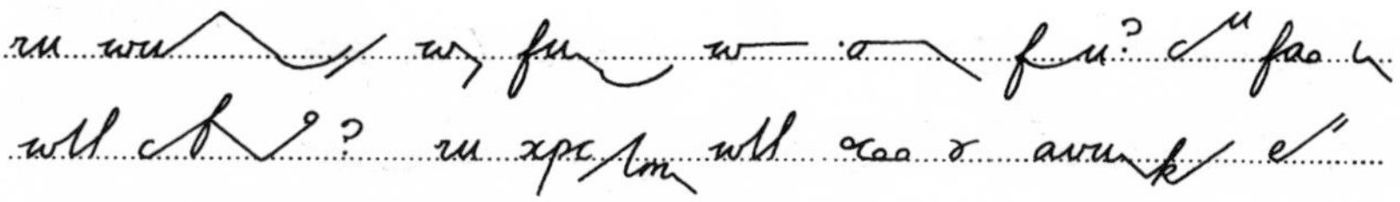

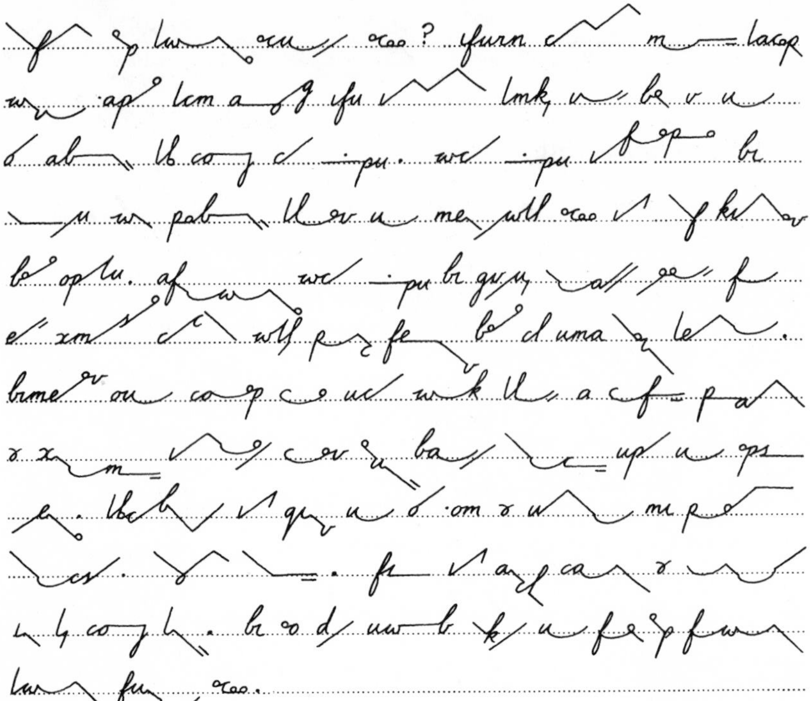

Dictation Passage 18

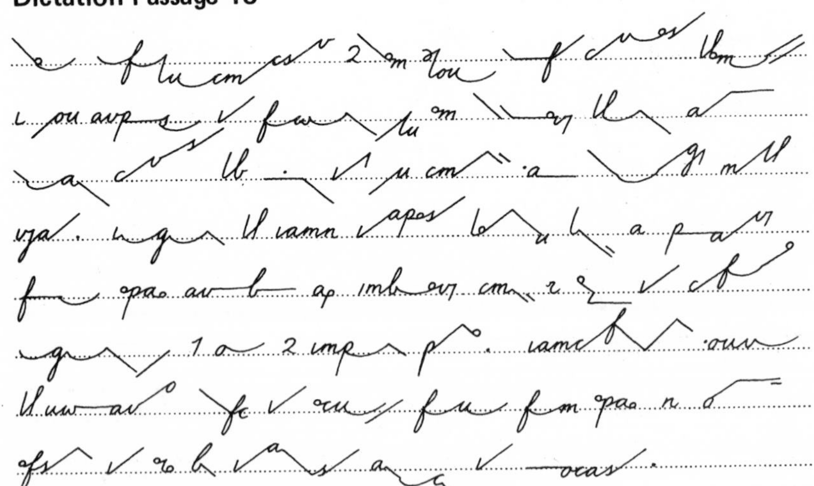

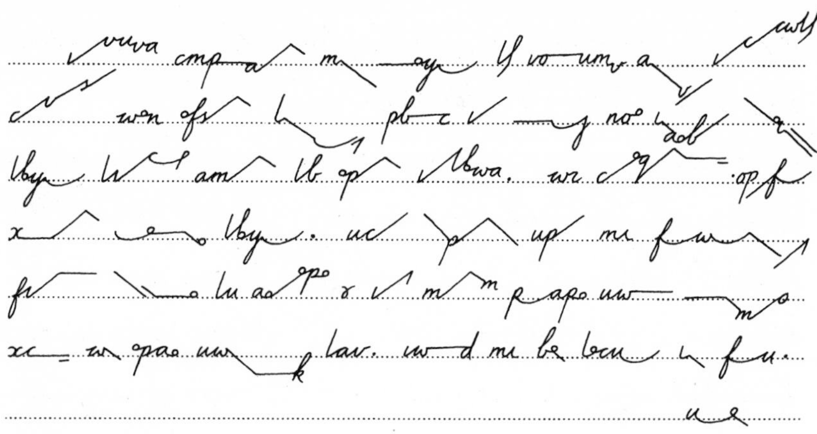

Dictation Passage 19(a)

Dictation Passage 19(b)

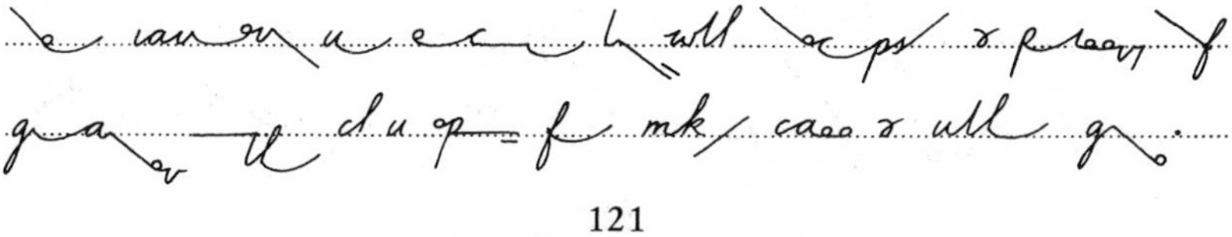

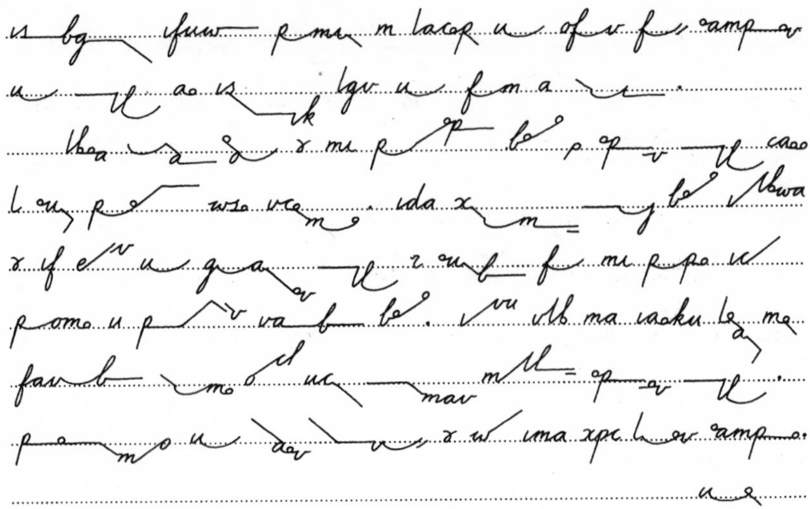

Dictation Passage 20

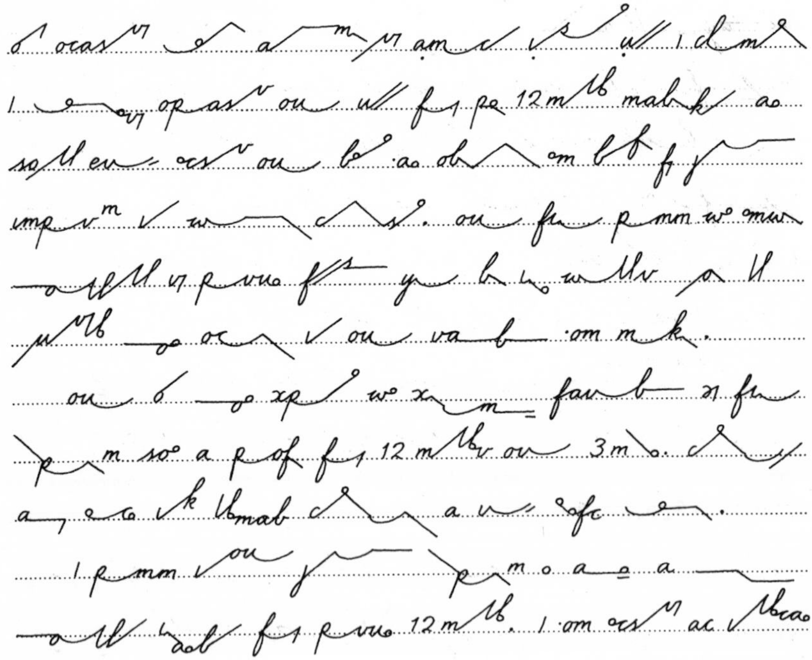

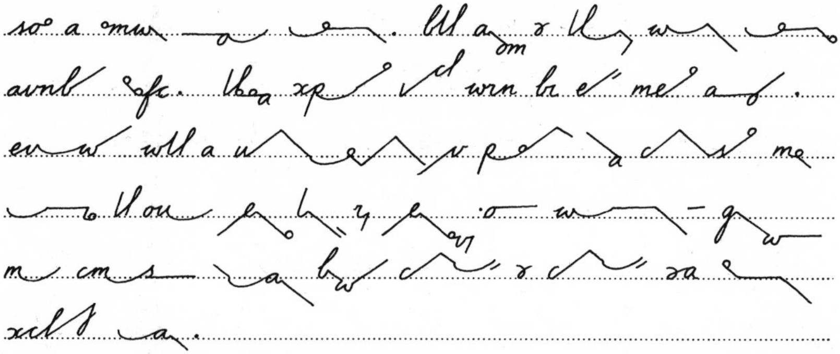

Dictation Passage 21

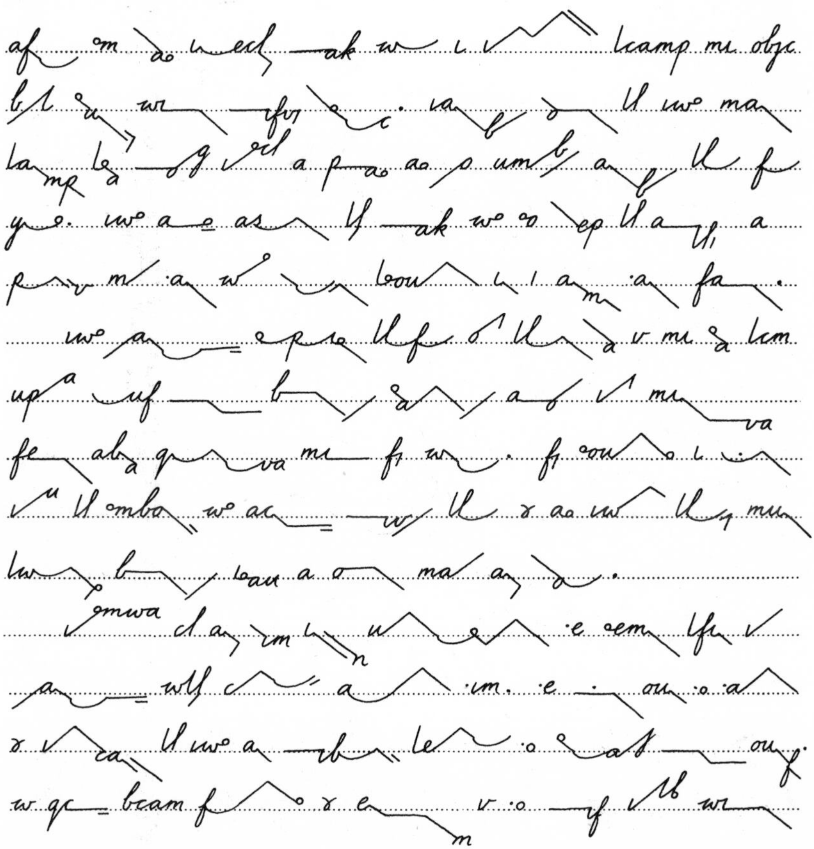

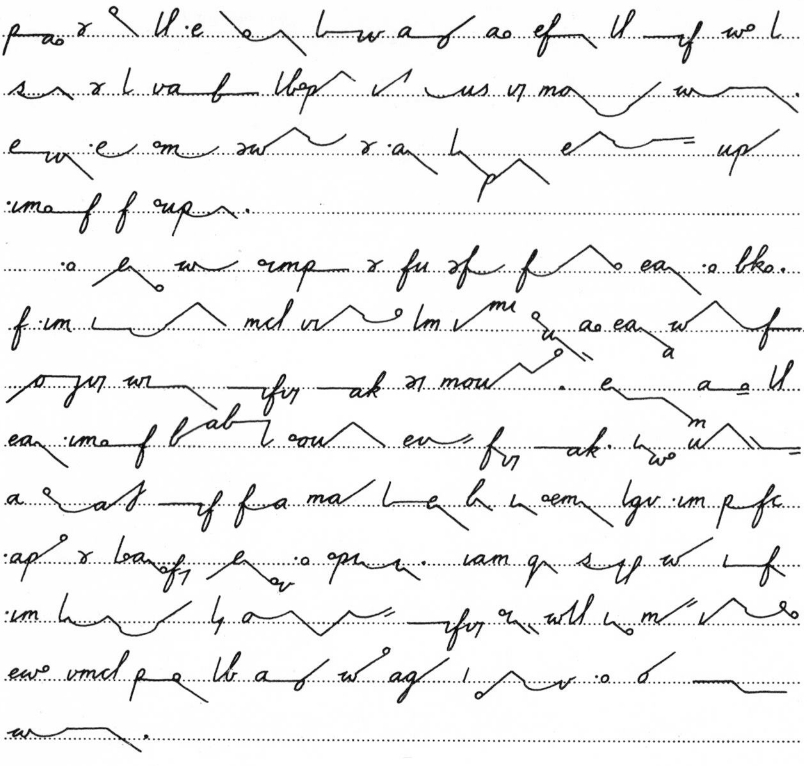

Dictation Passage 22(a)

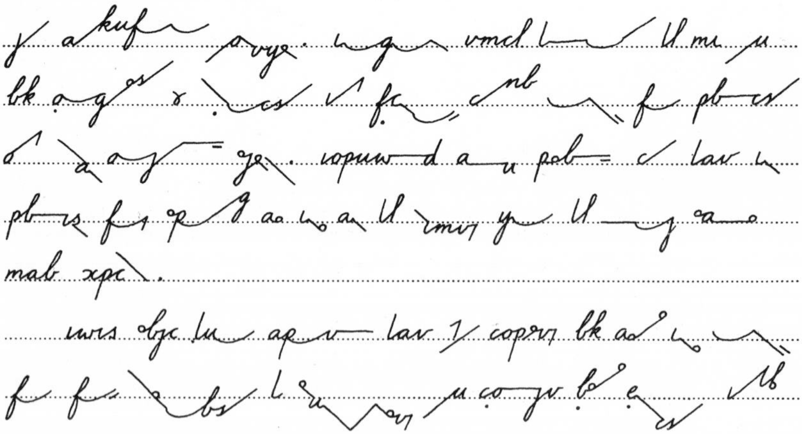

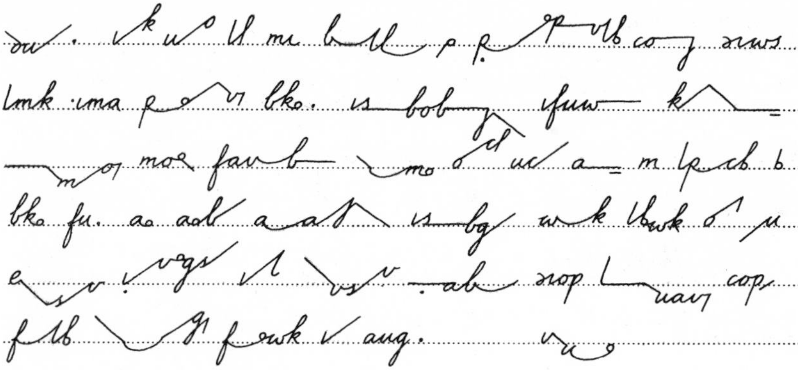

Dictation Passage 22(b)

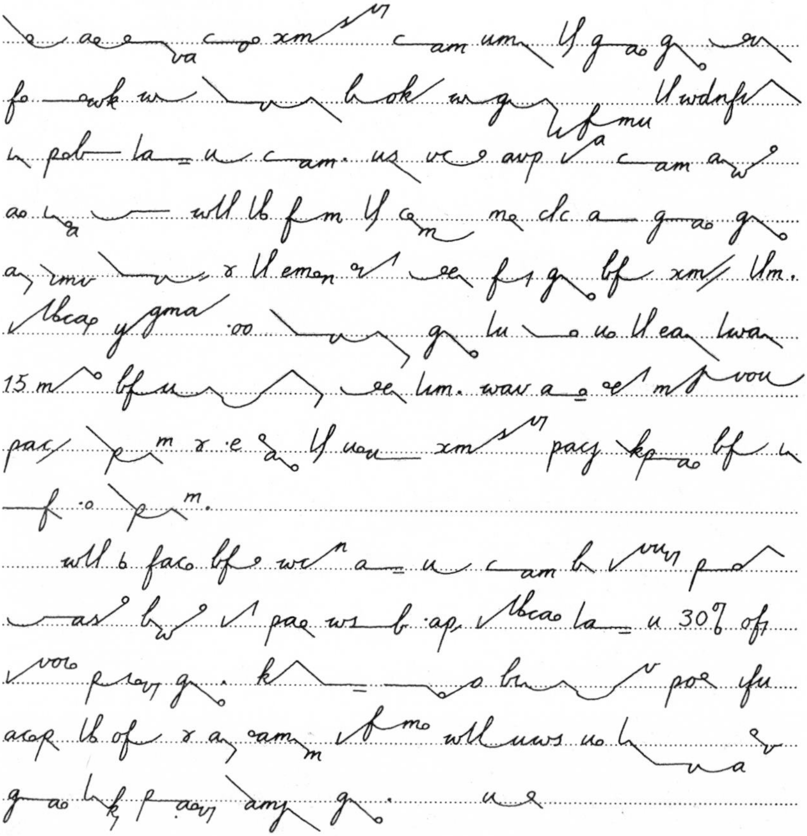

Dictation Passage 23

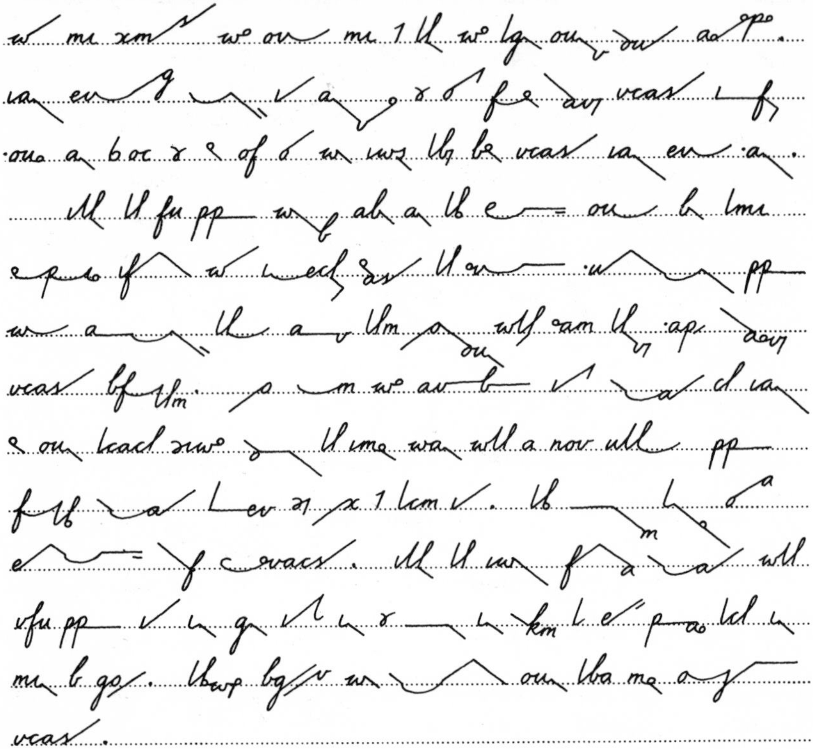

Dictation Passage 24

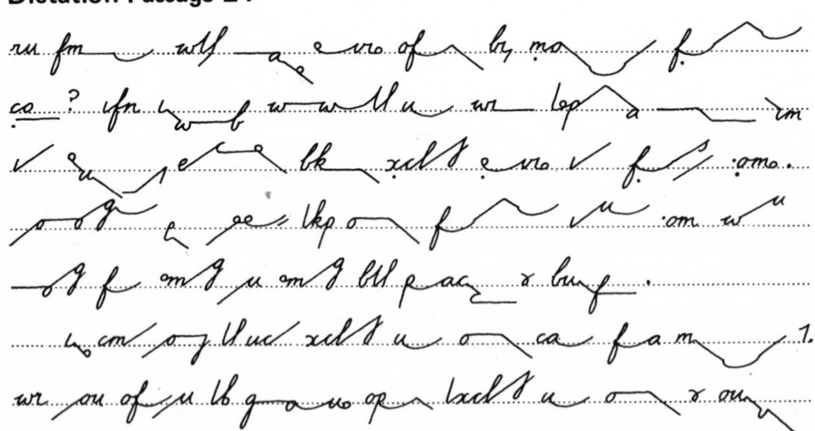

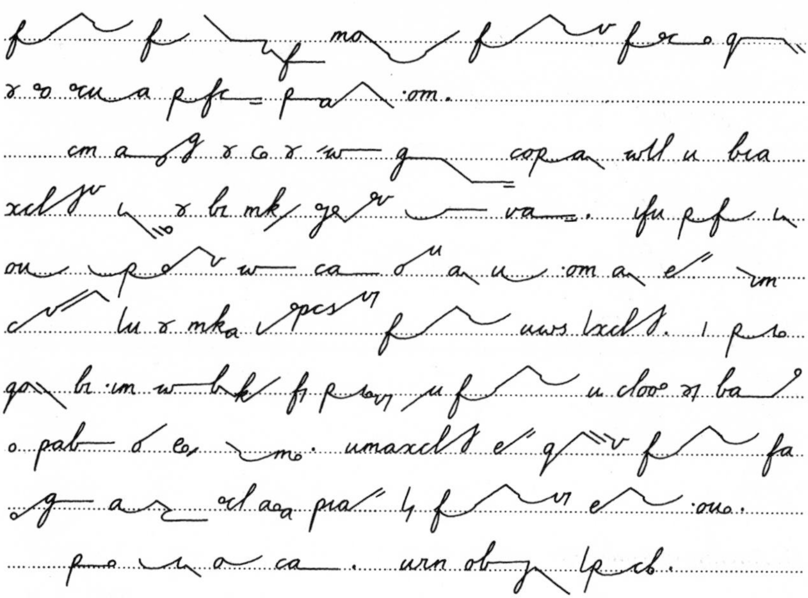

Dictation Passage 25

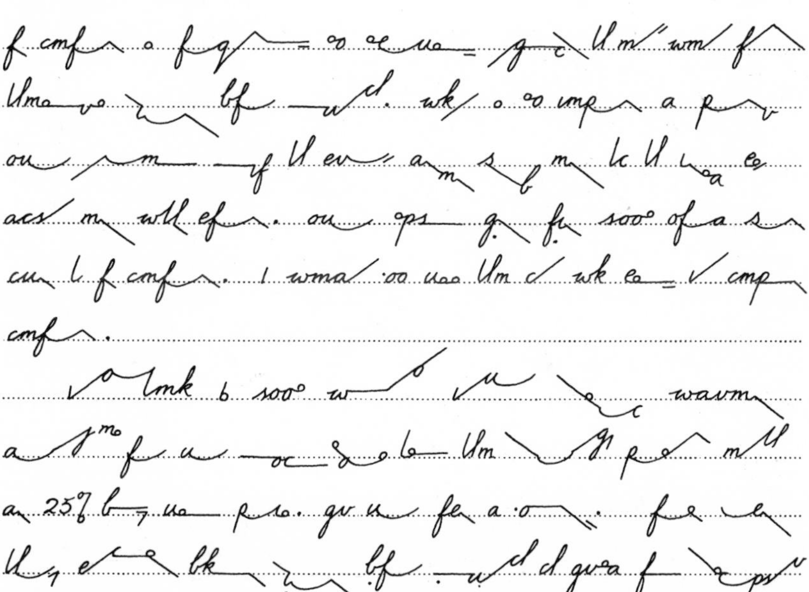

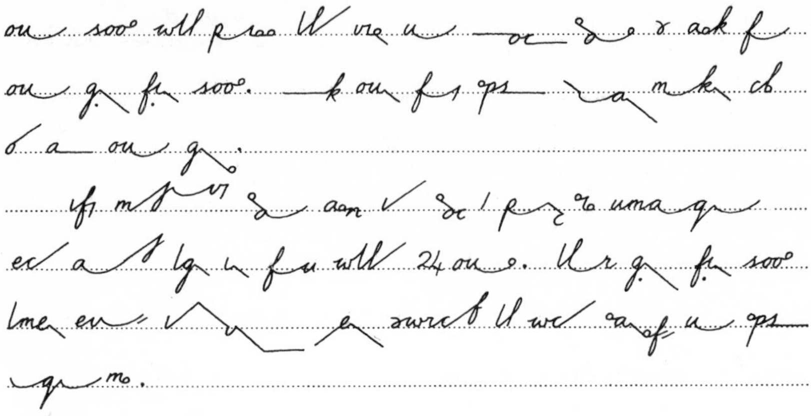

Dictation Passage 26

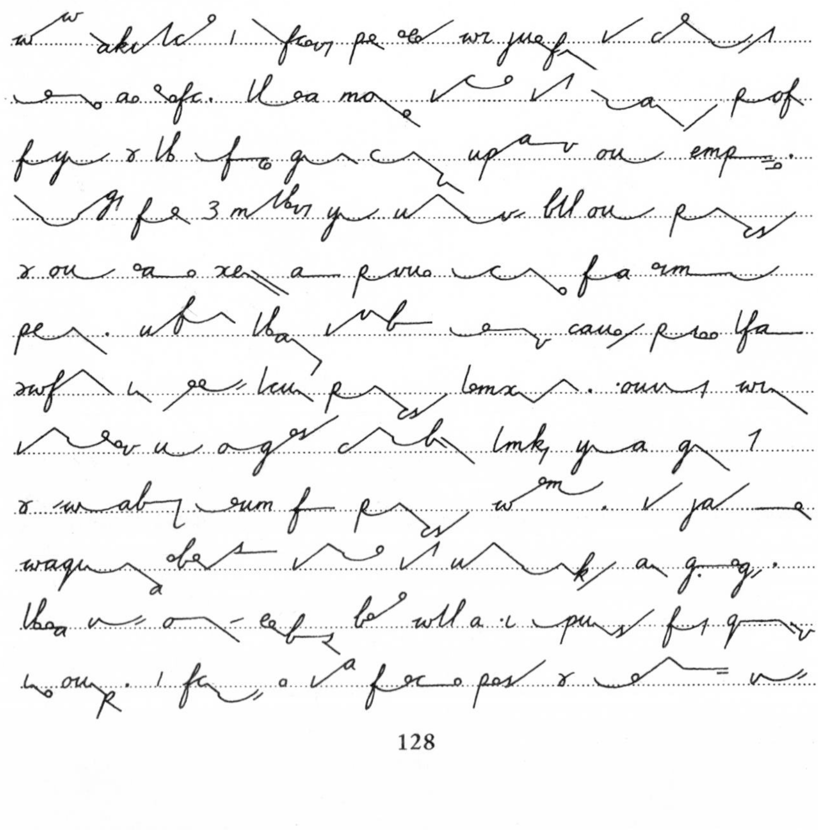

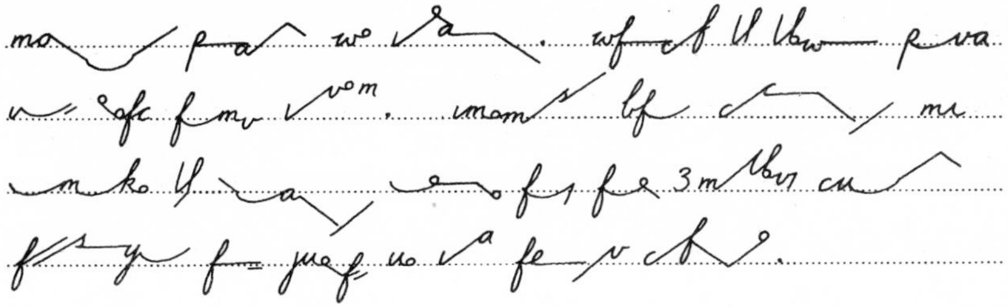

Dictation Passage 27

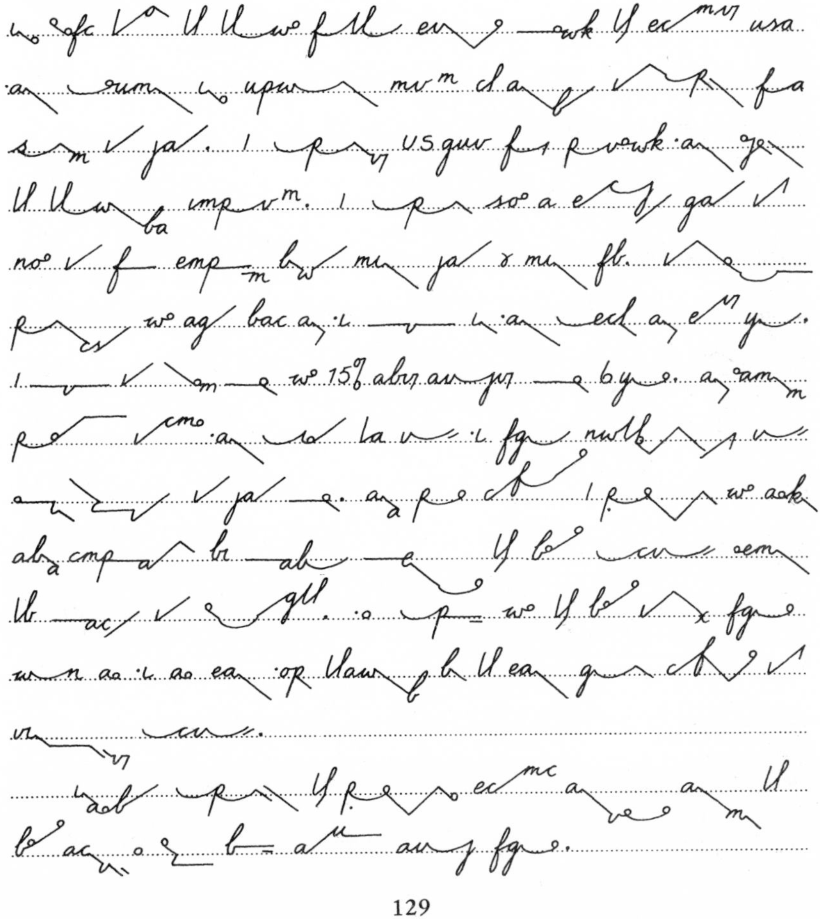

Dictation Passage 28

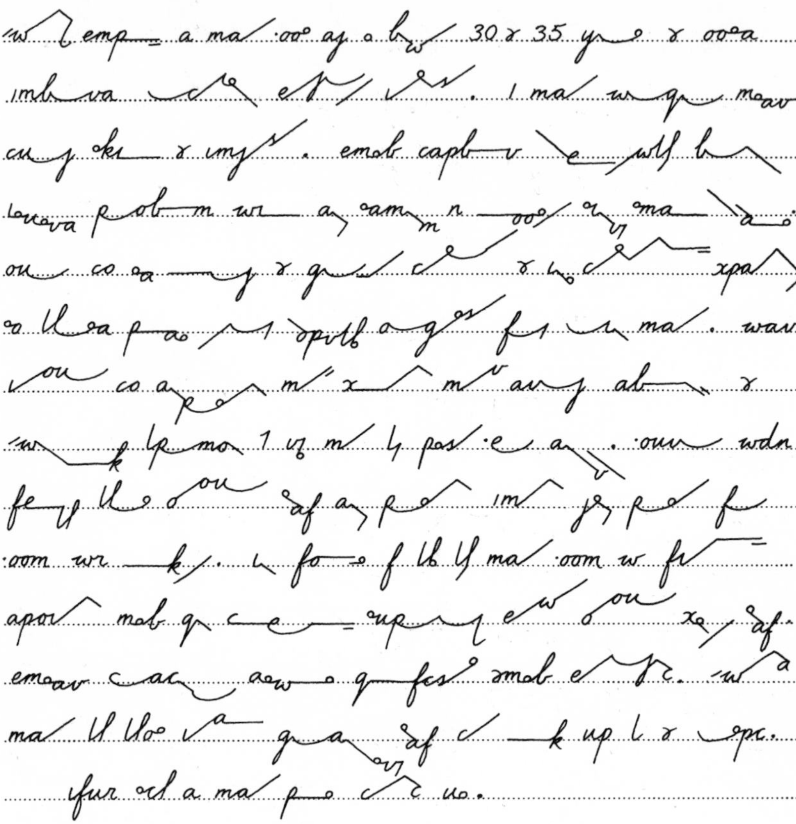

Dictation Passage 29

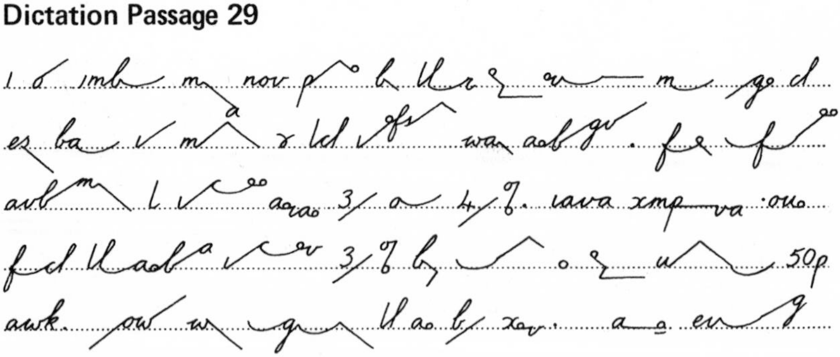

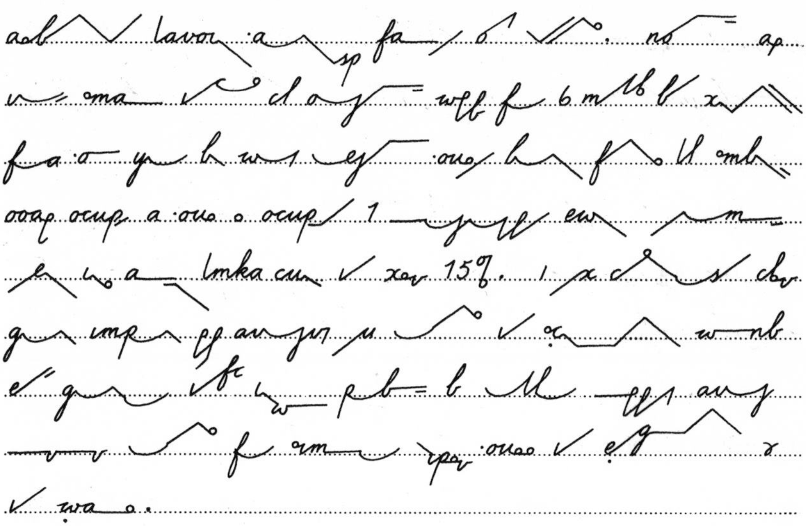

Dictation Passage 30

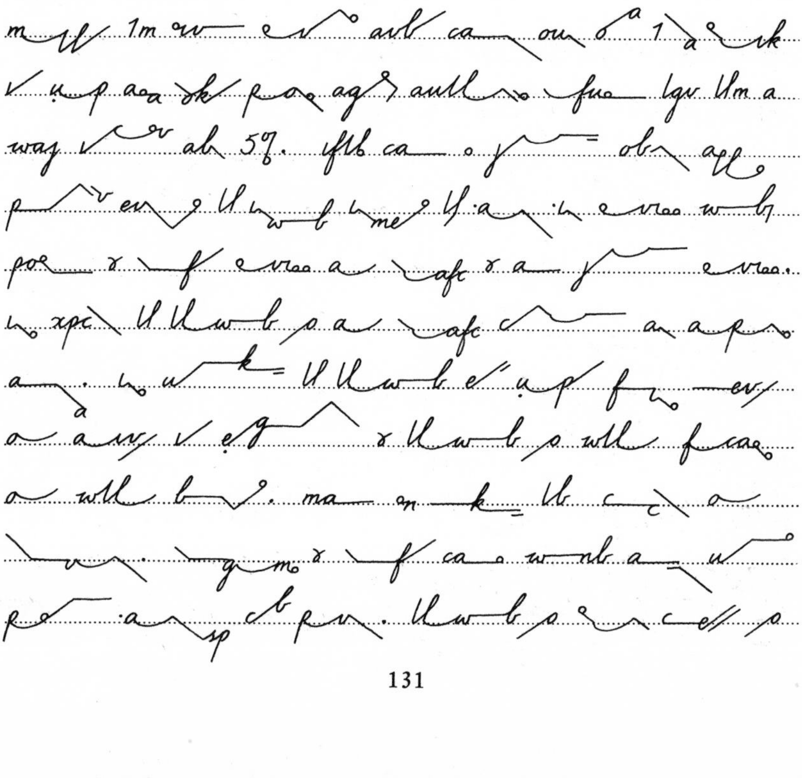

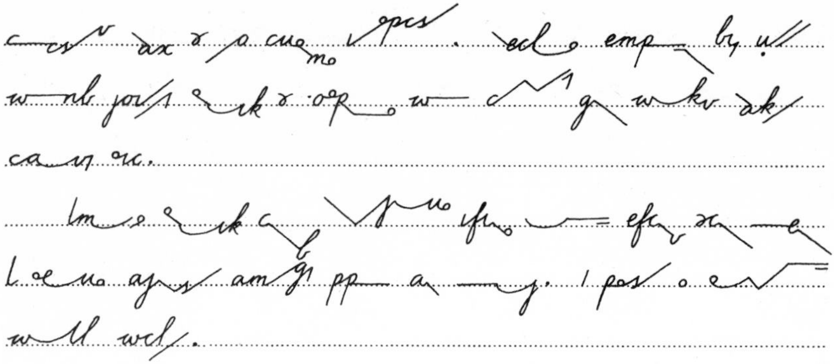

Dictation Passage 31

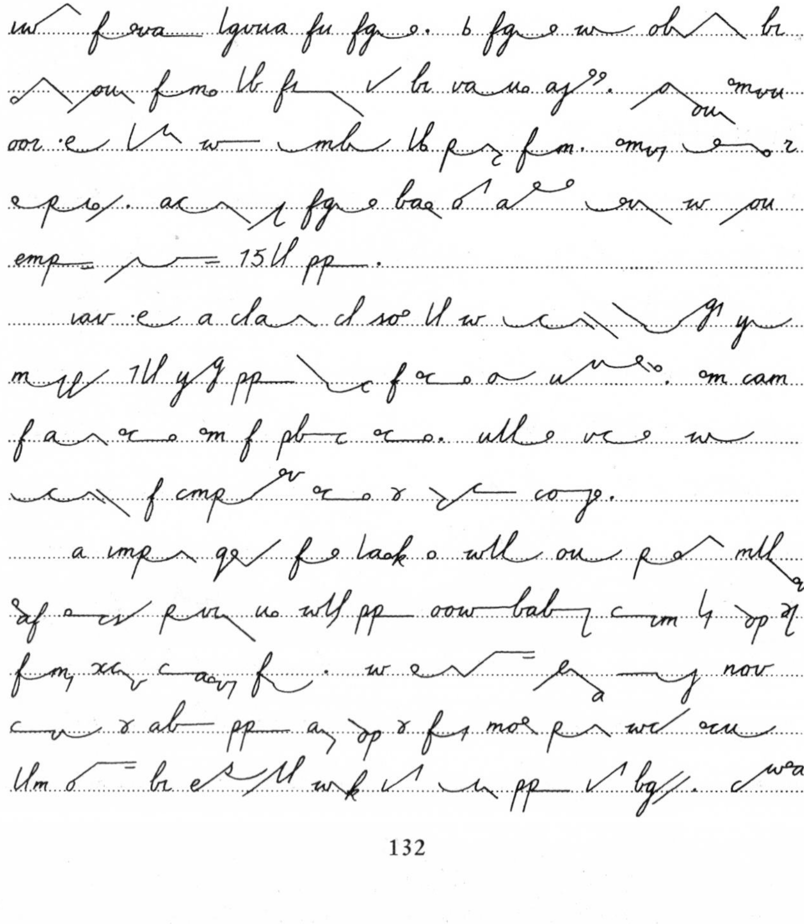

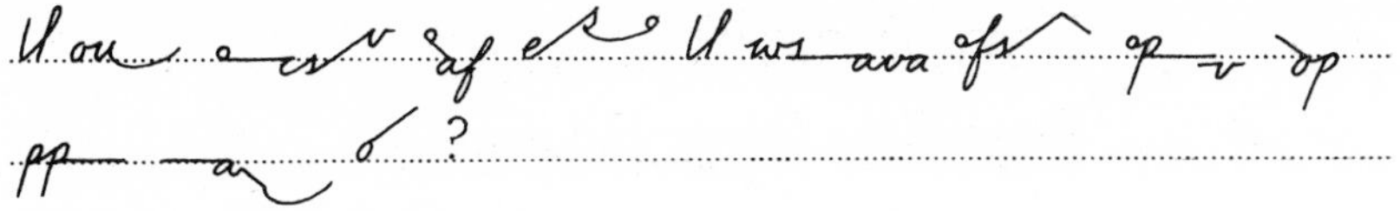

Dictation Passage 32

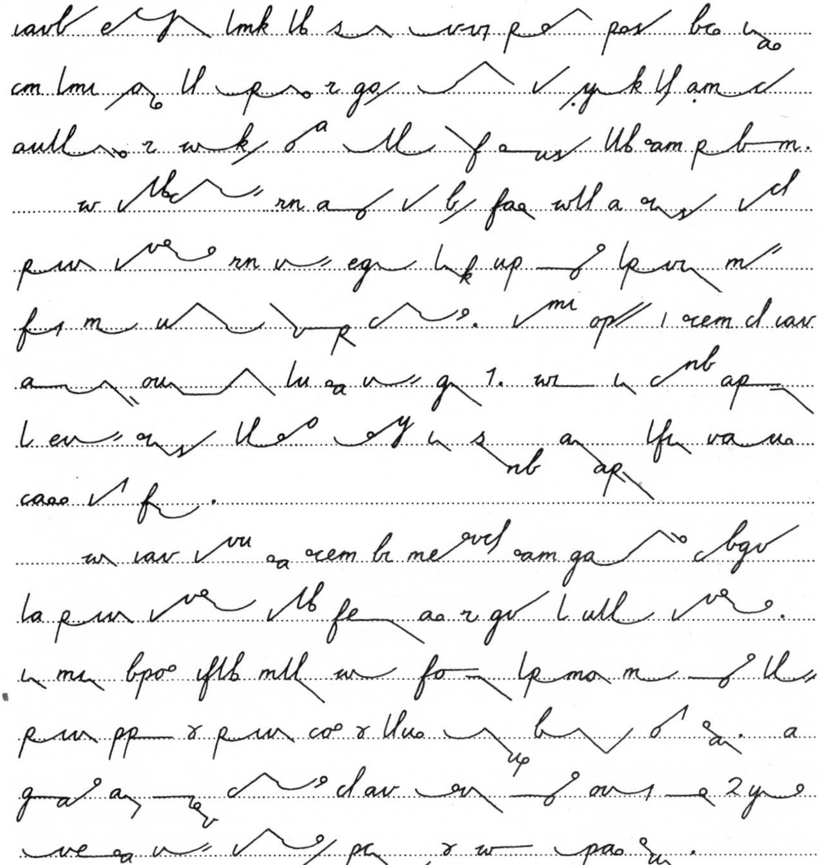

Longhand Keys to Facility Practices

Facility Practice 1

(a) our, ourselves, owe/oh, owing, plan, plant
(b) for, forward, work, worker, matter, material
(c) particular, particularly, instruct, instruction, instructions
(d) with regard to, in regard to, we regret, I regret
(e) we were, we were not, they were, they were not, you were, you were not
(f) to have, to have been, I have, I have been, you have, you have been, you have not been

Facility Practice 2

(a) official, officials, officially, out, outstanding
(b) person, persons, personal, personally, real, really
(c) be, between, improve, improved, improving, sit, situation
(d) I have, we have, I shall be, we shall be, very glad, very pleased, very much

Facility Practice 3

(a) custom, customs, customer, customers, accustom, accustomed
(b) late, later, latest, lately, quick, quickly, quickness
(c) part, parts, particular, particulars, particularly
(d) satisfy, satisfying, satisfied, satisfaction, unsatisfactory
(e) I sent you, we sent you, you sent me, will you send me
(f) and you must, and we must, and I must, so that, so that you are, so that we are

Facility Practice 4

(a) add, consider, addition, consideration, nation
(b) additional, national, ration, rational
(c) can, cannot, need, needs, necessary, necessarily
(d) I do, I do not, we do, we do not, you do, you do not
(e) next week, next week or two, next year, next year or two, next month
(f) I have, to have, I have been, to have been, to go, to get, to give

Facility Practice 5

(a) Sunday, Monday, Tuesday, Wednesday, Thursday, Friday, Saturday
(b) all, almost, also, already, all right
(c) nor, northern, more, morn, morning, mornings
(d) doubt, no doubt, to take, we take, I take, which is, which is not, this is, this is not
(e) owe/oh, owing, owing to, owing to the, due, due to, due to the

Facility Practice 6

(a) make, makes, making, manufacture, manufactures, manufacturing, manufactured
(b) river, rivers, Riverside, price, prices
(c) difficult, difficulty, difference, country, countries, county
(d) will you, can you, would you, if you will, if you can, if you would

Facility Practice 7

(a) expect, except, experience, experiences, experienced
(b) serve, serves, served, service, services, serviced
(c) require, requires, required, requiring, requirements
(d) we have, we have to, we have to thank, we have to thank you for your letter
(e) we shall, we shall be, we should, we should be, I shall, I shall be

Facility Practice 8

(a) Figures as shown
(b) Figures as shown
(c) 300, 3,000, 3,000,000, 300,000, 300,000,000, 3,000,000,000

Facility Practice 9

(a) train, trains, training, trained, transfer, transfers
(b) under, underneath, understand, understands
(c) this is, this week, this year, this month, this was
(d) to return, to try, to train, to murmur, to master

Facility Practice 10

(a) man, men, woman, women, manhood, womanhood
(b) relate, relates, related, relation, relations
(c) art, arts, heart, hearts, heartily, heartiness
(d) I was, I was not, I must be, I must not be, it must be, it must not be
(e) I know, you know, I knew, you knew, they know, they knew

Facility Practice 11

(a) north, south, east, west, eastern, western
(b) know, knows, knowledge, acknowledge, acknowledges
(c) after, afternoon, afterwards, aftermath
(d) exist, exists, existed, existing, existence
(e) it is, it is not, it is possible, it is not possible
(f) out of, set of, state of, couple of, pair of

Facility Practice 12

(a) today, tomorrow, yesterday, Monday, Tuesday, Thursday
(b) news, paper, papers, newspaper, newspapers
(c) direct, directs, directed, director, directors
(d) engine, engines, engineer, engineers, engineering
(e) matter of fact, matter of course, matter of interest, matter of opinion
(f) yesterday afternoon, tomorrow afternoon, this afternoon

Facility Practice 13

(a) outcome, income, outlet, inlet, outlets, inlets
(b) strong, strongly, strength
(c) on the, upon the, in the, into the, at the, for the, from the, of the
(d) to be, to be able, to be able to, to be unable to, able to, unable to
(e) course of events, course of affairs, of course, of course not

Facility Practice 14

(a) happen, happens, happened, happy, happily
(b) please, pleases, pleased, pleasure, pleasures
(c) I had been, he had been, you had been, we had been, there had been
(d) in the world, of the world, to the world, for the world

Facility Practice 15

(a) wish, wishes, wished, wishing, wishful
(b) success, successes, successful, successfully, succeed
(c) we have to, we have to thank you, I wish, they wish, we wish, and if I wish
(d) side by side, year by year, month by month, week by week

Facility Practice 16

(a) exam, exams, examination, examinations, examiner
(b) quote, quotes, quoted, quotation, quotations
(c) enclose, I enclose, we enclose, I am enclosing, we are enclosing
(d) ask you, we ask you, we must ask you, I shall ask you, please let us hear from you, for some time to come

Facility Practice 17

(a) excel, excels, excelled, excellent, excellence
(b) confide, confides, confided, confidence, confident
(c) secure, secures, secured, securing, security
(d) I meet, to meet, I make, to make
(e) can be, I can be, you can be, we can be, this can be, these can be

Facility Practice 18

(a) telephone, telephones, television, televise
(b) converse, conversed, conversing, conversation
(c) avail, avails, availed, available, unavailable
(d) referring to, I refer to, we refer to, in reference to
(e) as soon, as soon as, as soon as possible, as well, as well as, as well as possible

Facility Practice 19

(a) glass, glasses, grass, grasses
(b) special, specially, especial, especially
(c) accord, accords, according, accordingly, accordance
(d) leather, weather, father, feather, mother, brother
(e) let me, let me have, let me have your, let me have your reply
(f) you will, you will agree, you will agree that

Facility Practice 20

(a) insure, insures, insured, insurance, ensure
(b) premium, premiums, permanent, permanently
(c) commerce, commercial, commercially
(d) settle, settles, settlement, settlements
(e) annual meeting, annual meetings, annual report, annual reports
(f) 3 million dollars, 3 million pounds, 3 thousand dollars, 3 thousand pounds, 3 pence

Facility Practice 21

(a) lake, lakes, lakeside, actual, actually
(b) intend, intends, intended, intending, intention
(c) mount, mounts, mounted, mountain, mountains
(d) ordinary, ordinarily, extraordinary, extraordinarily
(e) I had, I had been, I have been, I would have been
(f) I see, I see that, I say, I saw, I saw you

Facility Practice 22

(a) organize, organizes, organized, organization
(b) fact, facts, factor, factory, factories
(c) depart, departs, department, departments
(d) thank you, thank you for, thank you for your, thank you for your letter
(e) let me have, let me know, let me say, let me finish

Facility Practice 23

(a) vacate, vacates, vacated, vacation, vocation
(b) hun, hunt, hundred, hinder, hindered
(c) catch, catches, match, matches, latch, latches, rich, riches
(d) I wish, I wished, we wish, we wished, I do not wish
(e) this is, this was, that is, that was, it is, it was

Facility Practice 24

(a) furnish, furnishes, furnished, furniture
(b) family, families, familiar, familiarly
(c) quote, quoted, quantity, quality, quantities, qualities
(d) no more, no less, no longer
(e) please let, please write, please let us know
(f) you may, you may not, you may exchange

Facility Practice 25

(a) show, shows, shoe, shoes, ship, shop, shadows
(b) arrange, arranges, arranged, arrangements
(c) describe, describes, described, description
(d) shall be, we shall be, should be, we should be, they should be
(e) you may wish, you may want, you may require, you may not
(f) in order, in order to, in order that

Facility Practice 26

(a) just, justify, justified, justifying, justly
(b) review, reviews, reviewed, reviewing
(c) require, requires, required, acquire, acquires, acquired
(d) conclude, concludes, concluded, concluding
(e) finance, finances, financial, financially
(f) for the year, of the year, in the year, by the year

Facility Practice 27

(a) further, farther, furthest, farthest
(b) upward, inward, downward, outward
(c) average, averages, averaged, averaging
(d) vital, vitally, vitality, futility
(e) UK, USA, ICI, IPB, FBI

Facility Practice 28

(a) merge, merges, emerge, emerges, energy, energetic
(b) nation, national, nationally, international
(c) promote, promotes, promoted, promotion, permit, permission
(d) we will, we were, we would, we want
(e) we do not feel, we do not see, we do not have, we do not like

Facility Practice 29

(a) hard, harder, hardest, hardship
(b) on/own, honour/owner, honours/owners, honourable, ownership
(c) refer, refers, referred, reference, references
(d) 400 per cent, 400 dollars, £400
(e) is the, is to, is not, is that, is this

Facility Practice 30

(a) like, likely, unlike, unlikely
(b) telephone, telephones, telegram, telegrams, television
(c) tax, taxes, taxed, taxation
(d) civil, level, evil, bubble
(e) 1,000,000, 2,000,000, 3,000,000, 100, 200, 300
(f) if you are, if he is, if we are, if that, if this

Facility Practice 31

(a) select, selects, selected, selection, selections
(b) agent, agents, agency, agencies
(c) 100, 1,000, 1,000,000, 500, 5,000, 5,000,000
(d) first of, first of all, more of, more than
(e) we say, can we say, we have, we shall have, we should have

Facility Practice 32

(a) encourage, encouraged, encourages, encouragement
(b) invest, invested, invests, investor, investment
(c) it cannot, it cannot be, there is, there is no
(d) can be, can be given, can be seen, can be done